CH01507972

We Should Expect a Spiritu

No man that warreth entangleth himself with the affairs of this life, that he may please him who hath chosen him to be a soldier.   2 Timothy 2:4

In the 1938 movie The Adventures of Robin Hood, Errol Flynn plays a dashing and courageous hero whose band of men hiding in the forest prevents the treacherous Prince John from taking control over England in the absence of good King Richard the Lionheart. Robin Hood steals from the rich Normans and gives to the poor and oppressed Saxons, wins the love of the beautiful Lady Marion, played by Olivia DeHavilland, and in the end kills the evil Sir Guy of Gisborne, played by Basil Rathbone, in a thrilling swordfight. In the movie, King Richard returns from fighting in a Crusade, joins forces with Robin Hood, and together they win the day and banish Prince John and his supporters to France. The movie ends with a large wooden door closing behind Errol Flynn and Olivia DeHavilland as they triumphantly leave the castle together arm in arm.

What is it about this type of story that captivates audiences from the day it first played on the movie screen down to our present day? The answer is that people simply love an exciting action story that pits good against evil, has a courageous hero who lives on the edge of defeat and death throughout the movie, and that resolves itself into a happy ending. Even Errol Flynn probably envied privately the fictional life of Robin Hood somewhat as he played it, with all of its daring escapes, courageous stands against injustice, unselfish sacrifice to help others in need, and most of all Robin Hood's fearless character that wins the admiration and love of the beautiful Lady Marion. As the common saying goes, "it could only happen in a movie."

But there is something else about this movie that tells us something important about ourselves. Few people, if any, want to know (other than idle curiosity) what happens in the lives of Robin Hood and the Lady Marion after the castle door closes behind them. Robin Hood vanquishes all of his evil foes, saves the day, wins the fair lady and that is the end of the movie and the end of our interest in the story. No movie producer in his or her right mind would do a sequel to The Adventures of Robin Hood in the aftermath of this movie, unless some screenwriter could come up with an equally thrilling tale having Robin

Hood and the Lady Marion again battling evil conspirators threatening England. An adventure-less movie that had Robin Hood dealing with the everyday life problems of managing the Nottingham Castle estates, like repairing the north gate, or checking on the water level of the castle moat, or planting enough barley in the south fields, would have people quickly yawning and heading for the theater exits in ten or fifteen minutes.

In the 1935 movie A Tale of Two Cities, staring Ronald Colman, based on the classic book by Charles Dickens, again no one cares what takes place in the loving home of Charles Darnay and Lucie Manette after their friend Sidney Carton sacrifices his life on the guillotine, during the French Revolution, to secure their future happiness. Sydney Carton uses a daring scheme to switch places inside the prison with the unjustly condemned man Charles Darnay, the husband of the woman Carton loves, and thus redeems his ill-spent life with a sacrifice so noble that it approximates on a smaller scale the death of Jesus on the cross for the sins of mankind. Yet as the horse-drawn coach carrying the saved family speeds away from Paris and towards England and safety, and Sidney Carton looks peacefully upward toward heaven as he climbs the steps to the guillotine, the movie comes to an end and so does our interest. The drama of the story with all of its interwoven themes and characters is resolved. After this we do not care that much about the everyday life of Lucie Manette and her family. As an audience we are not interested in the "they lived happily ever after" details of the story.

Coming up to a more recent time, the immensely popular movie Star Wars tells us the same thing. At the end of the final movie in the six-movie series, the fallen but reformed Darth Vader is burned on a funeral pyre, balance in the cosmic "force" is restored, Luke Skywalker and the Jedi are victorious, and Hans Solo and Princess Leia are finally together. The epic and adventurous parts of the story come to an end. Presumably all of these people then pursue a normal life after this, without having to battle the "dark side of the force."

What does this tell us about ourselves? If we could live our lives in the middle of a motion picture, what movie would it be and who would write the script? If we knew the story had a happy ending for us, would we really care how many adventures and narrow escapes we experienced to reach the conclusion? Would we want a boring script, or would we want the script writer to come up with something that was meaningful, inspiring, and even had some measure of risk and adventure? Would we be excited about even a small speaking role in an all-time great movie, as long as our character was well written and we knew we were part of something special and extraordinary? As Christians, these are questions we should be asking ourselves as we look at our own lives in relation to the lives of the people of faith in the Bible.

Errol Flynn was a great adventure actor, but he was not at the same time renowned as a screenwriter. The two men who wrote the screenplay for The Adventures of Robin Hood, Norman Raine and Seton Miller, were expert screenwriters but not famous actors. Ronald Colman was a great leading actor, but was not a good enough writer to come up with a story as great as A Tale of Two Cities. The screenplay for this movie was written by W. P. Lipscomb and S. N. Behrman, based upon the book written by the famous author Charles Dickens. *In all great motion pictures, the actors rely upon scripts and stories that are written by other people.* I am not aware of any great movie where the main actor also wrote the screenplay. An exception in recent times is the movie Good Will Hunting, co-written by Matt Damon and Ben Affleck, in which both have leading roles. At any rate, without screenplays, great actors would have no movies in which to act.

The Most Qualified Talent-Scout in the Universe

One of the themes that is hidden just below the surface of the lives of the people of faith in the Bible, which is clearly apparent once you see it, is that God wants to write the scripts and screenplays of our lives (Philippians 2:13). People like Noah, Abraham, Joseph, Moses, and David in the Old Testament, and Peter and Paul in the New Testament, put all of their hopes, dreams, aspirations, and even their lives on the line to follow the plans of God for them. God is able to write and direct real-world life-plans that are in most cases above and beyond fictional motion picture screenplays. God wants to write the scripts for our lives because He is simply better at it than we are, and He has an overall message He wants to get across. He wants the entire universe and all of creation to know that He is a trustworthy, capable, and loving God. The reading of the Bible and our own present-day Christian lives become more understandable once we grasp and embrace this concept.

All of us want our lives here on earth to count for something positive. Like our interest in a good adventure movie, we want the events and circumstances of our lives to be channeled toward some good conclusion. But like motion picture actors who are not screenwriters, we are incapable of coming up with plot-lines that also include trust, reliance, and faith *in a supernatural God.* To add these elements to our life-script, we need the great Screenwriter,

3

the God of the Bible, to compose imaginative lives for us like those of the people of faith in the Old and New Testaments. This is one reason why God inspired the writing of the Bible (2 Timothy 3:15-17). The Bible gives us an accurate pattern and template of what He accomplished in other people's lives so that we can also release our faith and have confidence in what He can do in our own lives. Only God has the divinely creative imagination to compose life-scripts for us that contain eternal purpose, meaning, and truth.

When people plan and manage their lives while pushing God away, they opt for the default screenplay for life. This default screenplay calls for the typical need for security, material possessions, the approval of friends and family, conformity to the conventional worldly pleasures of life, and usually putting as much distance as possible between ourselves and anything unpleasant in terms of character building. The problem with this approach is that the typical 60, 70, or 80 year old life here on earth is like a vapor of smoke (James 4:14) that is gone in what seems like no time at all. Before we know it, we can regretfully look back upon a life lived without purpose, meaning, or eternally beneficial impact upon others.

Sometimes a few exceptional people do manage to pursue exciting lives that have the outward appearance of challenge and adventure, but it is nonetheless on their terms and within the limits they set for themselves. Because we cannot live two parallel lives at the same time, the self-led and self-directed life, no matter how attractive according to outward appearances, is by definition a God-less life. There can only be a single plot-line for our character in the movie script of our lives. If self-absorption and self-centeredness is the storyline of our lives, then God's plan for us is pushed off the pages. We choose who writes our life-script...ourselves or God.

To have eternal satisfaction, purpose, and meaning, our lives must include God. A much higher purpose for life exists, which is described and recorded for us through the examples of the people of faith in the Bible. That purpose is to live out the fulfilling role that God has individually pre-written just for us in the great screenplay of human experience. If we do not allow God full participation in our lives to lead us into that divinely inspired role, because of timidity, fear, unbelief, self-centeredness, being too worldly busy, or thinking we know better than God, in the end we will be the person most disappointed.

After the ten plagues in Egypt forced Pharaoh to release the Israelites from bondage as slaves, it was God, through Moses, who led the Israelites to set

4

up temporary camp on the shore of the Red Sea. When Pharaoh and the Egyptians changed their minds, and pursued the Israelites with their chariot army, the Israelites were trapped by the Red Sea. This was God's doing. Moses had not made a mistake. He was listening correctly in the Spirit to God's voice.

When the Israelites saw the Egyptian army, they panicked. The Egyptian chariot army was not going to pull up to the crowd of Israelites and calmly discuss the terms of their return to Egypt as slaves. The Egyptians were going to massacre a large number of Israelites, in retaliation for what had recently occurred in Egypt, and then force the survivors back to Egypt. Although their lives were hard and bitter in Egypt, they still had had wives, children, enough food to eat, and a roof over their heads. At that moment the Israelites were wondering why they had given up their hard but secure existence in Egypt for the promise of freedom through faith and hope in a leader named Moses and in a God they barely knew. The circumstances were real, immediate, and they did not look good. The Egyptian soldiers had spears and swords they would soon thrust through the Israelite men, women, and children, without a second thought. Yet they were trapped by the Red Sea.

Unlike the fictional stories of *Robin Hood, A Tale of Two Cities*, or *Star Wars*, this author believes that God actually did place a real pillar of fire to temporarily block the Egyptian chariot army, and that God did open up an actual dry land passage through the Red Sea. I was not there. I did not see it happen. But I believe these were actual historical events. If God can create the physical universe out of nothing through the Big Bang, it should be relatively easy for Him to supernaturally open up the Red Sea and hold back the waters long enough for people to pass safely through. I know from the transformation that happened inside me when I accepted Jesus Christ into my life, and through several supernatural experiences of God's faithfulness in my life since then, that this is just the type of thing that God would do with the Israelites at the beginning of their history-making exodus from Egypt (Isaiah 14:24).

If Christians have experienced being spiritually reborn (John 3:3), then they personally know that God can supernaturally intervene in the affairs of mankind. Something extraordinary like the parting the Red Sea for the Israelites simply falls somewhere along the sliding scale of the magnitude of the various works of God.

Not Humanistic Invention, Myth, or Folklore

The issue that is contrasted here in this story of the Exodus, is the difference between play-it-safe security versus step-out-in-faith significance (Matthew 14:29). It is the difference between a risk-free life that accomplishes little of eternal value, and a bold life that purchases faith and trust in the living God that is worth more than gold. Either the God of the Bible is real or He isn't. Either God can be counted upon in a crisis, or He cannot. Either the Bible is true or it is a collection of fables. Unlike walking out of a theater after watching a fictional motion picture for two hours, every Christian can choose to follow Jesus through a real, actual life of faith, and discover and prove for ourselves whether or not our God is the same God we read about in the Bible. A true journey of faith with the God of the Bible is a testable proposition, with the real possibility of success or failure through situations large and small.

The Israelites could have continued living in Egypt, scratching out an existence with no purpose or meaning, or they could step out in faith and follow God. But in this defining moment in the separation of belief from unbelief, in the dividing of trust in the living God from self-sufficient existence in Egypt, there was a real *cost* to following God. God led them to the edge of the Red Sea.

It was God Himself who set up this life-and- death situation for the Israelites. In this make-or-break test, there was not enough time for any self-generated options for the Israelites. They could not set up an adequate defense, purchase weapons of warfare from surrounding nations, or send emissaries to hire foreign armies to come and help fight the Egyptians. At any moment, either they would be killed by the Egyptians, or God would somehow deliver them. Faith, trust, and reliance upon God were at the heart of this crisis.

We see from this example that it was the intention of God to initiate this final confrontation with the Egyptian army, so that God could demonstrate once again to Moses and to the Israelites His deliverance power and unfailing love. God knew that He could and would open up the Red Sea, and it appears that Moses also knew this from God sometime before it actually happened. It was the Israelites who needed to discover the depth of God's love for them, and He did this through a spectacular display of His power over nature, in the midst of this seemingly unsolvable dilemma. This was intended to provide the Israelites with hope and assurance to see them through the difficult days ahead and to provide us with a powerful example of hope we can apply today as well.

6

If we as Christians today believe the Bible is true, and that these events actually occurred, then we should not be surprised when God maneuvers us into similar situations and circumstances, albeit on a less dramatic scale, that enable God to reveal to us His deliverance power and caring love as well. This is how we grow. This is how we get spiritually strong. This is how we each individually get to know God better. This is how we become able to stand up spiritually on our own two feet and proclaim boldly what God has done for us.

God has not changed. He has an infinite variation of scenarios and life-scripts at His fingertips. We don't all have to play lead roles like Robin Hood, Sidney Carton, or Luke Skywalker, but God has a carefully chosen and well-intentioned role for each of us to play as mature and savvy Christians to make an impact for good in our world.

Some great novels are so captivating, that the reader dreads the book coming to an end. But as the pages turn one after another on a quiet Saturday afternoon, the last page is finally reached, the story ends, and the back cover of the book is closed. Some movies are so entertaining we wish they would go on and on. But these movies also end, the lights in the theatre come on, and people head for the exit doors.

After Jesus and the two thieves were taken down from their crosses, these blood-stained crosses presumably stood empty for awhile on Calvary Hill. Jesus, the Holy Spirit, and God the Father had accomplished their plan for Jesus to be the Lamb of God sacrifice for mankind's sin, slain from the foundation of the world (Revelation 13:8). The time of the actual crucifixion came and went, with Jesus then going on to rise the third day (Luke 22:37). Like an empty stadium after a championship game, or like an empty theater after an award-winning play or a virtuosic music recital is over, the time for the grand event comes and goes.

All of the upcoming end-times events are scheduled to occur in the near future. Jesus Himself talks about them in the gospels. They must happen. They are part of mankind's destiny. They were set in motion when Adam and Eve each took a bite of the forbidden fruit long ago. The story of good versus evil has been playing out ever since. Each of us has a part to play in that story.

We worship a real God who is both all-powerful and all-good, and who happens to also be a master screenwriter and director. We can surrender the course of our lives (Romans 12:1) into His hands with confidence, discovering first-hand His goodness and trustworthiness through our own individual experience of a walk of faith.

An old proverb aptly applies here: "a ship in a harbor is safe, but ships were not made for harbors." We were created for an adventure of faith, out upon the wide-open seas of life, following the life-script that the true and living God of the Bible has written for us.

Chapter Two

God's Optimum Training Program

I council thee to buy of me gold tried in the fire, that thou mayest be rich; and white raiment, that thou mayest be clothed, and that the shame of thy nakedness do not appear; and anoint thine eyes with salve, that thou mayest see. As many as I love, I rebuke and chasten; be zealous, therefore, and repent.

Revelation 3:18-19

A truly great high school football coach who cares about his players will work them hard during the late summer two-a-day conditioning drills. The football team that is heading toward a successful season can be heard groaning and complaining about the coach's tough training methods and seemingly impossible standards for the entire six to eight weeks leading up to the first game of the regular season. It is only after the team takes the field and discovers that they are well prepared to play high-quality football that they can look back at their coach's emphasis on physical conditioning and the constant repetition of the same basic plays over and over again until they finally got them right. The character lessons these players learned from their coach, about how to approach a particular challenge with intensity of purpose, hard work, and a will to never quit, often last them throughout their lifetimes, long after they stop playing football.

A God who asks little of us cannot have much of an impact upon our lives and can never be considered great. A compromised message from the pulpit tailored to please people will never inspire the type of commitment that will produce excellence of character in us. A book like this one, on the high standards of God in the end-times, to have real value must inspire committed Christians to continue forward on their present journey of faith, and to jolt less dedicated Christians out of complacency.

The story of the Bible is God's call to people to give their best, to surrender all to Jesus Christ in trust and faith. God is a spiritual coach who demands the very best, by setting up a rigorous training program of situations and circumstances for our benefit. He does this because He loves us enough to want to see us victorious on the playing field in the actual game of life. Dumbing-down and diluting the Christian experience to a more comfortable level, results only in mediocrity. The Holy Spirit would never inspire or condone "Christianity Light" (Acts 4:8). God is not and never has been interested in producing mediocre saints. That is why He gave us outstanding natural talents, abilities, and capacities, like His own. God created us in His image. That is why God says to us "Be ye holy; for I am holy" (1 Peter 1:16).

God is the great playbook writer of the lives of faith portrayed in the Bible. The reason that God wants to compose the playbooks for our lives is that He wants to set up a regimen of spiritual training where we can be challenged to give our all...the very best we have to give. In the area of assimilating godliness, which we initially know nothing about, we need a demanding coach to set up the program and to push us to our limits. We won't reach excellence in the area of Christ-like character on our own. Like learning to play championship football as a team, or learning to play classical piano at an advanced level, we need someone who is more knowledgeable than ourselves to show us the way and to push us toward a greater effort.

The truly great teachers, coaches, and role models in our lives obtain our total commitment to do our best because we sense that their demanding standards are based upon the fact that they really care about our development as people. The respect and sense of worth that is shown toward us through a coach or a teacher, who cares enough about us to demand our very best effort, will often inspire us to perform at our highest level for a lifetime.

Jesus said that He is the way, the truth, and the life. Jesus is telling us here that He has the winning play-book, and that He is the Championship Coach. Only God knows what it takes to have godly character. If we will join the team, and not quit, God will set up a tough spiritual training program for us. God does this because He cares about us. Like an inspiring college professor, a demanding high school athletic coach, or a respected parent, we will find ourselves wanting to please God and get His approval in everything we do.

That is the greatness of Jesus Christ. He inspires a life-long commitment to excellence in the course of our life. God takes people like Abraham, Joseph, David, and Paul, and transforms them into people with spiritual character and power in the areas of life that really matter. Abraham becomes the father of faith, Joseph leads the nation of Egypt through seven years of famine, David becomes a godly king, and Paul evangelizes the Mediterranean world. These are the world-class results when God is our coach and we submit ourselves to His program of spiritual conditioning and training.

10

The Easy Route Won't Produce Results

When we pick up our cross and are following Jesus, God is intimately involved with our spiritual training program. The cross and the resurrection of Jesus Christ set up this initial beneficial environment. Through Jesus, man can re-establish fellowship with God with a fresh start as new creatures in Christ. God the Father looks at us through Christ. Christians are sinless in the sight of God the Father through the blood of Jesus shed on the cross, *so that* we can experience a walk of faith through the situations and circumstances God composes for the believer in this life.

This program of spiritual training is extremely important to God. In the Old Testament, God was constantly fine-tuning, changing, and using the outward political environment to get the Israelites back into a relationship of trust and faith in Him. The various challenges of invading foreign armies, temporary military occupations of their homeland by surrounding nations, the powerful messages of prophets sent by God, and the Babylonian captivity, constantly re-established the correct environment for trust and faith in God for the Israelites during their long history. The letters to the churches in the New Testament are designed to keep Christians within the purity of an environment of faith and trust in Jesus Christ.

As always, Lucifer attempts to get Christians off course by subverting and attacking the God-composed environment created for faith and trust to operate. Lucifer's strategy is a straight-on attack at the very program that God sets up in this physical world designed for the people of faith to discover His love and His care.

If Lucifer incites the Midianites to attack Israel, God responds with the calling of Gideon and the uniquely creative plan of the counter-attack with the 300 Israelite soldiers. This re-established an environment in Israel for active faith in God. If Lucifer incites the Philistines to invade Israel and defy the God of the Jews through a warrior champion like Goliath, God counters with the raising up, seemingly out of nowhere a courageous young man named David. David kills the giant with one sling-shot stone perfectly aimed into the forehead of Goliath. This starts in motion a process to establish the reign of a godly king in Israel that sets up the environment for the Jewish nation to again exercise trust and reliance upon God.

The scriptures tell us that Lucifer desired to "sift" Peter during the faith-testing period of the arrest and trial of Jesus (Luke 22:31), to destroy Peter forever in self-incrimination and despair over failing to remain true and faithful to Jesus at the critical moment. Lucifer successfully uses the unfamiliar, intimidating surroundings of the home of Caiaphas the high priest, as an unanticipated and underestimated new environment for Peter, who utterly fails in courage to acknowledge Jesus before a group of people assembled around a fire in the exterior courtyard. Yet God counters by using this very same crushing defeat in Peter's life to create a life-changing character transformation in Peter, from previously being foolishly self-confident and self-reliant to becoming humbly and wisely reliant upon the Holy Spirit for the remainder of his life.

Lucifer attempts to discourage and weaken Paul's resolve for service by inciting a near-death stoning of Paul by the Jews at Lystra. Lucifer tries to bring disruption and doubt into Paul's calling, to bring in an element of fear and possibly unforgiving resentment and bitterness toward the Jews into Paul's God-inspired program of evangelizing the Greco-Roman world. Instead, this failed attempt by Lucifer to attack the ministry of Paul probably only created more spiritual freedom in Paul's outlook.

From that time forward Paul could consider that he was now operating on borrowed time. Paul had looked a horrible death square in the face, and got up and carried on. If Jesus Christ could raise Paul up from this stoning experience at Lystra, what more could Paul have to fear from opposition to his ministry? Paul could look at each current threat and say to himself that he already experienced far worse and had survived. But on a deeper level, 1 John 4:18 says: "but perfect love casteth out fear." This extreme physical attack upon Paul did not dampen his love for his Jewish brethren (Romans 9:1-3). Paul exhibits fearless ministry in perfect love (within human limits) throughout his calling to evangelize the first century world, because Paul stayed faithfully within the rigorous training environment that Jesus Christ set up for him. No matter what was occurring in the natural realm in terms of the deadly malice and hatred of the opposition, Paul remained steadfast.

These are all examples of a great, championship-quality Coach instilling the high standards of character and preparedness that produce victory on the field of play.

The greatest harm that man can do to the ways of God is to tinker with the training environment of faith that God sets up. Man is constantly trying to replace the spiritual training program of a walk of faith with God, with empty religious practices that homogenize, sanitize, and nullify the environment of situations and circumstances whereby God can interact with faithful believers. This occurred throughout the Bible. It starts with the lethal contrast between Cain and Abel. Cain wants to change the rules to suit himself. Cain wants to do things his way, with deadly tragic consequences.

In the New Testament, replacing God's ways with our ways is one of the underlying causes of the lethal differences between the Jewish religious rulers and Jesus, which culminated in the crucifixion of Jesus the Son of God. There is no basis for the extreme outcome of the crucifixion of Jesus the Lamb-of-God-sacrifice for the sins of man in the first century, if there are not deadly stubborn and hard-hearted hypocrites sitting in the seats of power as religious rulers in Jerusalem. The religious leaders of that day, and Jesus and His disciples, are in two totally different realities, two different character-building programs, two different spiritual "training camps" that are worlds apart. This difference is what fueled the tension that finally resulted in the crucifixion of Jesus.

The Pharisees, Sadducees, scribes, and lawyers did *not submit themselves* to the spiritual equivalent of the grueling two-a-day August workouts that typically lead up to the start of the high school football season, orchestrated by a demanding coach getting his team into top physical shape to be winners on the football field. The ministry of Jesus Christ exposed the fact that they had not gone through God's spiritual training program. Otherwise, they would have recognized the voice of God their divine Coach during the Sermon on the Mount. They would have been conspicuous within the crowd, with heads nodding up and down in agreement with what Jesus was teaching, walking in amongst the audience patting people on the back and encouraging them to listen to what the Master was saying.

Instead, Luke 11:52 reads: "Woe unto you, lawyers! For ye have taken away the key of knowledge; ye entered not in yourselves, and them that were entering in ye hindered." The ministry of Jesus exposed the fact that they were outside of the uncompromising environment of faith that God sets up for the benefit of all. Jesus exposed the Pharisees and scribes as unskilled and untrained players, posing as qualified players in the starting line-up on the field, and they killed Him for this (Matthew 27:18).

13

When the Pharisees and Sadducees came to John the Baptist at the river Jordan, John said "O generation of vipers, who hath warned you to flee from the wrath to come? Bring forth, therefore, fruits befitting repentance" (Matthew 3:7-8). In other words, John the Baptist said "show that you are genuine athletes prepared for real play on the field, and not just pretenders and frauds wanting to wear the uniform during the game, and wanting to walk around campus wearing the varsity jacket during the week."

The context of situations and circumstances in which God sets up faith and trust to operate, is not a matter to be taken lightly. God and Lucifer are in a constant spiritual battle over who controls the territory of the environment of situations and circumstances. The Exodus of the Israelites out of Egypt, and the method of preparation for them to be able to conquer their promised land, is a straightforward biblical example of this concept. God took Israel out of the context of Egypt and into the Sinai desert. God changed the environment altogether. In the desert God had more exclusive access and control of outward situations and circumstances to craft lessons of trust and reliance upon Him. The external issues for the Israelites in the desert were narrowed down to the basics …food, water, and getting the memory of Egyptian idol worship out of their thinking.

In the desert God was able to get the undivided attention of the Israelites, and to get them trained in the spiritual areas of trust and reliance upon Him, so that they would follow Him and Joshua into the all-important impending military battles. God did not want the Israelites to be terrified at the first sight of warfare. God wanted the Israelites to march forward into battle with determined resolve and courage, for their own benefit and welfare. God's demanding and challenging training methods with the Israelites, at the very real risk to Himself of becoming temporarily unpopular, proved to be of the highest championship quality.

Lucifer, by contrast in this environment of the Sinai desert, had fewer tangible outward opportunities to work with. The usual glittering worldly temptations and allurements were not present in the desert. Spiritual military "boot-camp" provided fewer openings for Lucifer to operate within.

One of the fallacies that should be addressed as we approach the upcoming end-times is the idea that just because we are born-again Christians, God is satisfied with spiritually out-of-shape and overweight players on His team. This idea of a soft brand of Christianity is not biblical.

14

Every born-again Christian will be raptured when the time comes, regardless of what shape we are in. The thief crucified next to Jesus, who that very day would be in paradise with Him, with no future opportunity to live out his new faith on earth, tells us that salvation is entirely by grace through faith and not conditioned upon works. But the idea that Jesus Christ will not set up a rigorous training environment to get us all into top spiritual shape before the end, whatever particular eschatology the end-times may entail, needs some serious re-thinking within contemporary Christendom.

This current environment of earth is a one-time, non-repeating event. The end-time is the last "football" season for all eternity. Jesus Christ will not allow His team to go out with a losing final season, because we were out-of-shape, unprepared, and poorly coached. The perfect, divine coach Jesus Christ unselfishly loves each one of us too much to allow that to happen.

Chapter Three

A Fourth Cross on Calvary Hill

Looking unto Jesus, the author and finisher of our faith.   Hebrews 12:2

One of the basic messages of the Bible is that God's ways are higher and better than our own. This is one of the pivotal, fundamental lessons of the Christian experience. Only the real, supernatural God can compose and direct circumstances in our lives that will lead to genuine, everlasting spiritual growth. It is within God's unique character- manufacturing furnace of present-time experience that He forges mature saints who can trust and follow Him. Peter and Paul are two of the best examples of this process from scripture.

Before the crucifixion, Peter thought (according to Peter's understanding in the realm of the "natural man") that Jesus was in peril from the Jewish leadership in Jerusalem, and that Jesus needed Peter's personal help for physical protection (Matthew 16:22). When Peter utterly failed in this capacity, to the point that he actually denied knowing Jesus using cursing to save himself out of a difficult situation in the courtyard, Matthew 26:75 says: "And he went out, and wept bitterly." Peter was not just mildly disappointed in himself. He thought he had failed in the critical, defining moment in his life.

But this was not the defining moment in Peter's life. God the Father knew from eternity past that Jesus would die on the cross, and that He would raise Jesus from the tomb of Joseph of Arimathaea. God did not need or want Peter's help to prevent the crucifixion of Jesus. That was merely Peter's best intentions according to his own thinking. *The critical moment that God* had planned for Peter was not at the midnight trial standing alongside Jesus as a faithful companion, but on the Day of Pentecost in Jerusalem, at the birth of the Christian church, as described in the second chapter of the book of Acts.

On Resurrection Day, when Peter first sees the risen Jesus (1 Corinthians 15:5), Peter realizes in an instant that God did not need his well-intentioned help to guide these final events. God did not need Peter to prevent what Peter thought would be a guaranteed negative outcome if Jesus fell into the hands of the Jewish authorities. God the Father had raised and transformed the broken and mutilated body of Jesus Christ the Son from the effects of a violent death that had occurred only a few days before, into a new and glorious resurrected body. In a moment of realization, in the light of finally understanding, it all comes together for Peter.

Peter thinks back upon Jesus by the lakeside, in a boat because of the press of the crowd, as He is brilliantly teaching truth like no one has ever heard before (Luke 5:3). Peter remembers the oversized catch of fish in the nets that nearly overturns Peter's boat (Luke 5:4-11), the miracle of the feeding of the thousands on the hillside (Matthew 14:15-21), Jesus walking on water (Matthew 14:22-36), the transfiguration (Mark 9:2), lepers cleansed (Luke 5:12-15), the blind receiving sight (John 9:1-41), and the dead raised (John 11:1-44).

When Peter intently gazes upon his risen Lord on Resurrection Day in amazement and appreciation, he cannot take his eyes off Jesus. He realizes in a series of quick flashbacks the always up-to-the-challenge Son of God, working masterfully with the Father and the Holy Spirit through every imaginable human issue and crisis, but especially in this final, amazing, unexpected event of salvation for mankind through the bodily resurrection of Jesus after the seeming finality of death on the cross. Peter realizes that Jesus had Peter's denial in the courtyard factored into the whole process all along (Matthew 26:34). With an enormous sense of relief, Peter now understands that his personal failure at the critical time…when under normal circumstances Jesus might have otherwise needed his support the most…that any well-meaning attempt on the part of Peter to physically protect Jesus could not possibly have prevented or affected in any way the monumental work of salvation planned by Almighty God so long ago.

Peter was also resurrected to an eternal hope in that single moment of time upon first seeing the risen Jesus (1 Peter 1:3). In a bright flash of spiritual light, Peter in that instant finally realized that God was infinitely bigger than he was. Peter saw with his own eyes the capacity of God to overcome anything, no matter how hopeless, when he saw the risen Jesus. This experience changed Peter forever.

At that moment Peter shifted his reliance from self to God. Peter could go forward from that day onward with the rock-solid hope of a living faith, and a vessel emptied of self-reliance, to serve his Savior to the end of his life. This is how Peter was able to stand up before thousands of people in the center of Jerusalem during the celebration of Pentecost, through the power of the Holy Spirit, and not through his natural leadership ability and bold personality, to successfully proclaim the truth that Jesus was indeed the Christ of God.

Peter's prior overconfident statement, before Gethsemane, that even though all other men might forsake Jesus, that Peter under no circumstances would forsake Him (Matthew 26:33), revealed a person who was still partially self-led. Peter was talking out of his un-crucified self-in-charge nature, and this led to bitter spiritual defeat. Peter, in the courtyard of Caiaphas the High Priest, was not operating "in the narrow gate" (Matthew 7:13-14) of listening to and following the Holy Spirit, as an apostle of Jesus Christ should. Trouble found and exposed a vulnerable flaw in Peter, because self was still in-charge in this instance. The character transforming lesson of Peter's denial of Jesus in the courtyard, and the loving forgiveness he experienced in his personal interview with Jesus on Resurrection Day, changed Peter from self-led failure to a Spirit-led overcomer. Peter's encounter with the risen Christ is an example of experiential faith that actualized into spiritual victory.

Rewinding these events backwards in time, Peter could have faithfully and courageously stood at the side of Jesus, as he said he would, and been condemned to death as a follower of Jesus. Peter would then have occupied the fourth cross on the hill of Calvary that Passover Day.

But God the Father had a much different plan for Peter. How infinitely better and more exciting would it be, to be filled with the Holy Spirit on the Day of Pentecost, and to stand up before thousands of people in Jerusalem and preach powerfully about both the crucifixion and the resurrection of Jesus Christ the Messiah (Acts 2:14-36)? How much more exciting would it be to bring Tabitha back to life (Acts 9:40), or to heal the crippled man at the gate to the Temple (Acts 3:7), or to participate in the revival in Samaria (Acts 8:14-25), or be preaching to the Gentiles when the Pentecost "gift of the Holy Spirit" was poured out on them as well (Acts 10:44-48), or be miraculously released by an angel in the dead of night from Herod's prison (Acts 12:7-11)?

How much better was God's plan for Peter than what Peter had in mind for himself prior to the arrest of Jesus in the Garden of Gethsemane? To what purpose would a fourth cross on Calvary, bearing Peter, have served? According to historical tradition, Peter was eventually crucified in Rome, sometime in the early 60's A.D. Peter was finally crucified physically, but not before living a full life in service to his Lord Jesus Christ according to the much higher plans of God.

The Narrow Gate for Paul (Matthew 7:13-14)

Paul's appeal to Caesar in Acts 25:11 is another excellent biblical example of God's foresight and intervention in guiding the fine details of the lives of people who are in the midst of a walk of faith with Jesus Christ.

Paul is under arrest in Caesarea for the tumultuous uproar that occurred in Jerusalem. Paul does not know that the sympathetic Roman ruler, King Agrippa, will arrive in Caesarea in the near future. Agrippa apparently would have released Paul (Acts 26:32). The Jewish authorities want Paul to be returned to Jerusalem for trial. Paul knows that there are forty Jews sworn to attack his escort of Roman soldiers conducting him back to Jerusalem, but even if Paul makes it safely back, any hearing in Jerusalem would be prejudicial against him. But Festus, the Roman official having jurisdiction over Caesarea, suggests in an open hearing, for political reasons, that Paul be brought to Jerusalem to be judged before Festus regarding the accusations against Paul. Before Agrippa arrives, Paul has no choice but to appeal to Caesar.

This is a fascinating and instructive development in the story of Paul. It provides all Christians with a window into how God works in our lives if we will follow Him completely and not lose faith. As events narrowly unfold in this account of Paul in Caesarea, Paul is compelled to appeal to Caesar for a hearing in Rome. This changes the entire nature of the ministry of Paul from being a man of action planting new churches in Asia Minor, to a man with quiet time to contemplate and compose the upcoming "prison epistles" written while in Rome (Ephesians, Colossians, Philemon, and Philippians).

At this late stage in Paul's career, more new churches in Greece and Italy are probably not needed. History shows that the number of churches in existence when Paul set off for Jerusalem for the last time, were enough in number and quality to create a strong foothold for the spread of Christianity in the first century. If left up to Paul, he would have continued to faithfully pursue his original calling, traveling and planting new churches in Greece, Italy, and he hoped even in Spain (Romans 15:24). But it was the God-appointed quiet time in Caesarea and in Rome that enabled the writing of these crucial last epistles to the churches that completed his inspired New Testament contribution of Christian doctrines and practices.

It is also this abrupt change in plans that provides the narrative story for the distinctly different final four chapters in the book of Acts, providing us with a look into the customs of Roman public hearings, an ancient shipwreck, and Luke's unfinished history of Paul in Rome that enables conservative scholars to date the ending of the book of Acts as a milestone event sometime in the early 60's A.D. This has enormous apologetic value in validating the authenticity of the New Testament gospels in relation to the activities of Paul, placing the gospel of Luke and the book of Acts so close to the time of the ministry of Jesus as to remove the possibility of legendary development or exaggeration entering into the New Testament. It took God intervening in the situations and circumstances during this period of Paul's detention in Caesarea for this change-in-mission to occur. Through these tightly inter-related events, God closed one door and opened another door in the ministry of Paul.

The lesson here for every Christian is that no matter how fierce are the winds and the seas of the storm of circumstances around us, the eye of the hurricane is in the center of God's will. God sets up, guides, and molds events in the life of Paul, above anything that Paul could manufacture on his own, which results in the optimum final outcome for a life that is totally and completely surrendered to Jesus.

What is uniquely instructive about this episode in the life of Paul is that after this final visit to Jerusalem, he is under Roman arrest for most of his remaining years. Not only is solitude imposed upon him for the purpose of quiet reflection about all that he has learned and experienced, but Paul is also made safe from the external threat of harm that he daily lived with while he was out on the road, from the Jews or from any of his other enemies. Tradition does say that Paul was released for some period of time in Rome between a first and second imprisonment.

But from Caesarea onward, Paul was for the most part within God's bubble of protection through the use of Roman officials and the Roman judicial system. Paul could not be safer (other than eventual martyrdom by Nero around 62-64 A.D.) in the Roman world of the first century than to be under house arrest in Rome in the care of a Roman soldier. Paul no longer had to worry about hostile Jews from a previous city showing up suddenly, with deadly intentions, in the city he was currently ministering in (Acts 13:50; Acts 14:5; Acts 14:19; Acts 17:5; Acts 17:13; Acts 18:12; Acts 19:26).

Through the clarity of hindsight, we see that God accomplished two things at the same time…a change in the nature of the ministry of Paul, and the protective environment for Paul to compose his final letters to the churches.

This is a clear-cut demonstration of the narrow gate that Jesus is referring to in Matthew 7:13-14. It is an example of the benefits and outcomes that God would like to perform in our lives through experiential faith.

The Character Manufacturing Furnace

Nearly every Christian can look backwards in time and say: "Now I understand why God took me through that trial." Every Christian looks forward to the future with hope that we will improve as people and that things will get better. It is the *present time* that we all have difficulty with.[1] Knowing, without a doubt, that we have surrendered and yielded our lives to Jesus Christ, and that the present situations and circumstances in our lives are not an accident but are in the control of God, is a mark of the mature Christian. The mature Christian can apply every line of Psalm 23, along with David, with full assurance and confidence to their lives.

In-the-moment, present-time situations and circumstances is the furnace where Christian character is manufactured (James 1:2-4). Our self-in-charge natures will not venture anywhere near the character-manufacturing furnace. Self-in-charge is terrified of *the risk of potential failure* that is associated with this furnace. In the furnace of present-time, in-the-moment situations and circumstances, the issues are so important according to outward appearances that a real spiritual test is set up. Is God reliable enough to place my faith in as the Lord and Sovereign King of my life, in the present-time circumstances, or do I have to take matters into my own hands because the issues are simply too important to trust to anyone but myself alone (1 Samuel 13:12)?

This is a fundamental, pivotal issue of faith outlined for us throughout the Bible. Gideon was in the present moment when he went to battle with 300 men against tens of thousands of the enemy. David was hunted by Saul in-the-moment. Queen Esther made her decision to risk personal safety, in-the-moment, in approaching the King and opposing Haman to save her people from destruction. God told the young prophet Jeremiah not to be afraid of the countenance of the people's faces when Jeremiah delivered God's message to them, thus declaring plainly that it took some courage on Jeremiah's part to be God's spokesman. This challenge for Jeremiah occurred in-the-moment.

---

[1] Bob Mumford, Fifteen Steps Out (South Plainfield, NJ: Bridge Publishing, Inc.) 5-7

In the New Testament, Peter and John defending themselves before the Sanhedrin in Acts 5:29-32, had the very real risk of being stoned to death like Stephen a few chapters later (Acts 7:58-59). These accounts are all variations of the central question of the reliability of God's character in the fiery trial. These people all put their faith and trust in God in-the-moment of their present-time circumstances, thus declaring that they believed that the character of God was trustworthy.

The Holy Spirit is charged with the task of taking us to the character-manufacturing furnace of personally tailored situations and circumstances, but only if our self-in-control nature is subordinate to the will and plans of God. Any attempt to skirt around the Christian character-manufacturing furnace is self-deceiving. Certainly God is not fooled. God is only dismayed and hurt that we do not trust Him enough to let go of self-in-control. When we exercise faith and trust in God in the present-time, no matter what is happening or how bleak the circumstances look, we are saying we believe in the goodness and reliability of God's character.

The furnace of in-the-moment situations and circumstances is always a test of character, both God's and ours. This is where the value of a real relationship with the living God rises to the fore. It is not some homogenized, new-age diluted humanistic slogan like "let go, let god." People who say and teach these kinds of cleverly reduced, cheerleader-type motivational phrases generally have no actual intention of stepping down off the thrones of their lives and following the Holy Spirit into real-life circumstances that require genuine release and trust in the one living God.

The cross is difficult. Death to self-in-charge is not easy. Whether it is financial challenges, family issues, health struggles, or the opposition of people to our Christian ministry, God will set up the issues in our lives specifically to create this furnace of character-manufacturing for our spiritual growth. That is why the outward appearances of some of these situations and circumstances are frightening and terrifying. Without the genuine challenge of real consequences that matter, the decision to follow God would be too easy. If the Christian life went perfectly smooth from beginning to end, we would never learn anything about ourselves, about eternal truths, or about God.

Chapter Four

Spiritual Pride Needs a Context

But so shall it not be among you; but whosoever would be great among you, shall be your minister; And whosoever of you would be the chiefest, shall be servant of all.   Mark 10:43-44

For it to surface, spiritual pride needs a suitable context in our Christian life. In Mark 9:33-37 and in Luke 9:46-48, the story is told of the apostles disputing as they traveled on the road, who should be the greatest among them. They knew by then who Jesus was. They knew that they had been chosen to be the apostles of the Messiah the King. They suspected that events were coming to a head and that somehow Jesus would take His rightful place as the leader of the Jewish nation. They knew this opened up opportunities for them to occupy positions of leadership in Jerusalem. This new reality occasioned the dispute among them as to who should occupy the highest positions in the new upcoming kingdom.

This internal debate amongst these men could not have happened a few years earlier, outside of the context of their becoming apostles and disciples of Jesus. The thought of who would be the greatest among them in God's upcoming kingdom on earth, which they mistakenly thought would be politically established in the very near future in the capital city of Jerusalem, could not conceivably have happened while they were ordinary fishermen, tax collectors, or revolutionary zealots. Only after successfully following Jesus for two or three years as apostles and disciples did this tempting context materialize into a foreseeable eventuality.

Matthew 20:20-28 tells the story of the mother of James and John coming to Jesus and asking Him if her two sons could sit on His right hand and on His left hand in His kingdom. This request could not have been made without James and John being in the inner circle of apostles close to Jesus. The extraordinary ministry of Jesus created high future expectations among His followers for the nation of Israel. This provided the context for this forgivable and understandable ambition on the part of the mother of James and John.

Jesus did not rebuke the mother of James and John for this request (He probably inwardly admired the courage of her advocacy for her sons), but simply answered that she did not clearly understand the thing she was asking of Him. The scriptures then say that when the other ten apostles heard what the mother of James and John had done, they did not get upset with her but they were "indignant" against James and John.

The response that Jesus has for the apostles arguing among themselves as to who should be the greatest was to take a child and set him as an example in their midst, and tell them that "he that is least among you all, the same shall be great" (Luke 9:48). The apostles and disciples learned this important lesson well, and had the right spirit regarding this issue in their first century ministries. After these specific lessons by Jesus, and after the Last Supper when Jesus washed the feet of the apostles (John 13:2-17), we do not hear anything more about who will be the greatest among the apostles or disciples.

But the events of the crucifixion and resurrection of Jesus, in place of a worldly coronation and political reign in Jerusalem, also removed from the apostles the previous context of determining who would have high positions in the supposed new government. The first century church of new converts was the actual kingdom that resulted from the ministry of Jesus, not the worldly reign of Jesus the political King in Jerusalem. In the context of the New Testament church, Jesus' teachings about the least being the greatest, Jesus washing the apostle's feet, and Jesus using a young child as the example of the correct attitude for spiritual leadership, now made perfect sense to the apostles.

Luke 20:46-47 reads:

46 Beware of the scribes, who desire to walk in long robes, and love greetings in the market places, and the highest seats in the synagogues, and the chief rooms at feasts.

47 Who devour widow's houses, and for a show make long prayers, the same shall receive greater condemnation.

When the apostles disputed among themselves who should be the greatest, they were on a parallel road in terms of attitude with these scribes. Although they did not realize it, they too were similarly thinking about wearing long robes, being greeted as "somebody" in the market place, having the highest seats in the synagogue, and occupying the chief rooms at festivals. The sinful pride side of their natures was showing itself in this dispute, on account of the context of the possible upcoming rulership of Jesus in Israel. This would have

24

been the beginning of church leadership personality conflicts, power structures, political intrigue, and unholy ambition in the Christian church.

That is why Jesus took the time to speak to them about this important issue on several occasions. *And that is why, in God's infinite wisdom, He produced a different context for His bride the church from what the apostles had in mind as they disputed on their way to Jerusalem who would be the greatest.* God had in mind the humble New Testament church that could evangelize the world without the burden of worldly ambitions and concerns. The three thousand new converts on the Day of Pentecost would need church leaders who were humble shepherds and "servants of all", not self-important people more concerned with their outward appearances, titles, and reputations like the scribes of Luke 20:46-47. In Peter's speech to the multitudes on the Day of Pentecost, there is not a hint about himself, or about any personal ambitions regarding what he plans to do or to build in Jerusalem. Everything in Peter's message is about Jesus, and about people coming to Christ through faith. Peter is no longer thinking about having drapes measured for his large corner office in the Temple. Peter is fishing for men according to his true calling (Mark 1:17), not fishing for financial donations to build something.

The Pride of Life is Not of the Father (1 John 2:16)

What gets people into trouble in terms of pride is that they want more than Jesus. Human nature wants Jesus plus worldly recognition and acceptance. We want Jesus plus the moniker of outwardly visible success. The problem with a genuine biblical walk of faith with God is that *there isn't anything honorable, pure, holy, or commendable* beyond Jesus. Wanting more leads to the dispute of the apostles as they journeyed toward Jerusalem as to who should be the greatest. At that precise moment in time, the apostles possessed Jesus in the form of an intimate, accessible, physical person more than anyone has enjoyed in history. Yet they wanted more according to their fallen human natures. This character flaw had to be corrected if the new Christian church was to survive, flourish, and grow.

Paul honestly admitted that there was a part of him that "would desire to glory" (2 Corinthians 12:6). In Romans 7:15-25, Paul talks about the conflict of his two natures, the one that delights in the law of God after the inward man, and the other that attempts to bring him into captivity to the law of sin in his members. Also in Romans 12:3, Paul warns "every man that is among you, not

25

to think of himself more highly than he ought to think, but to think soberly, according as God hath dealt to every man the measure of faith."

John 7:17-18 reads "If any man will do his will, he shall know of the doctrine, whether it be of God, or whether I speak of myself. He that speaketh of himself seeketh his own glory; but he that seeketh His glory that sent him, the same is true, and no unrighteousness is in him."

For every Christian who is serving God in some capacity, there is a daily decision or bent of the heart to seek His glory and/or our own glory. The Holy Spirit reveals to us the spiritual pride that would tempt us to take what God has provided to us in terms of wisdom and light to use for our own glory. How do we rid ourselves of this tendency to seek recognition, attention, and acclaim for ourselves? The answer is to constantly remind ourselves to ask God to give us the strength and wisdom to "seek His glory that sent us," to stay within the parameters of our mission as agents of the King, to stay within our calling as servant-leaders.

The context within which we live and work has a lot to do with how well we can resist the urge to dispute along the road who should be the greatest, and conversely how well we can focus instead upon being a "servant to all." Being caught up within the center of God's plan for us provides the protective context that wards off destructive spiritual pride. Being focused upon God's leading takes our eyes off ourselves.

Every person has to examine his/her own motives. When the Holy Spirit puts a person forward as a preacher, evangelist, prophet, scholar, teacher, Christian movie-maker, or writer, then God is present to provide the measure of humility that is needed. This is what He did for the apostles after they disputed who would be the greatest. The last thing that God wants is for a Christian to reach the level of being able to serve and then fall to the temptation of spiritual pride that brought down Lucifer. Entering in at the narrow gate (Matthew 7:13-14) does not allow for Jesus plus worldly validation, acceptance, or acclaim. Our mission is to allow Jesus to glorify Himself in and through us in whatever we do. The correct spiritual equation of a walk of faith, is Jesus minus the need or desire for worldly recognition, validation, or acclaim. Unappreciated, unnoticed, thankless, humble, under-the-radar-screen service to God, when possible, is the safest spiritual place to be in Christian ministry.

Did Peter or Paul have to deal with the "advanced billing" of an exalted reputation that preceded them when they traveled to a new city to teach and preach? Of course they did. That is the reality of human nature. The city at large may not have heard of Peter or Paul, but the local Christian church looked forward with anticipation and "pride" that a great apostle (someone who had personally seen and heard Jesus Christ) was coming to speak to them.

Paul tells us how he stayed focused with the correct attitude. He told the Corinthians: "For I determined not to know any thing among you, except Jesus Christ, and him crucified" (1 Corinthians 2:2). Paul told the Galatians: "But God forbid that I should glory, except in the cross of our Lord Jesus Christ, by whom the world is crucified unto me, and I unto the world" (Galatians 6:14). Paul actually says in 1 Corinthians 4:9 that God "hath set forth us, the apostles, last" in order to establish and maintain a humble context of evangelical outreach, starting at the bottom floor of the social scale, allowing for the broadest possible sweep of lost sinners into the kingdom of God.

Nearly every Christian at some time or another has heard the phrase or the concept "empty vessel for God's use," meaning that a person has been prepared by God for some type of ministry or service. But the question can be asked, empty of what? The answer is all of the things that prevent a person from being able to be used effectively by God---pride, self-will, arrogance, haughtiness, fear, self-centeredness, impatience, being judgmental, racial prejudice, social prejudice, personal ambition, and many similar things. All of these attitudes in some measure or another hold back people from being filled with the Holy Spirit power and anointing to minister the gospel to other people.

The Christian disciple who is empty of self and open to service, has stepped off of the throne of their heart and allowed Jesus Christ to take His rightful place there as God. Like a small child (Matthew 18:2), the Christian who is walking in faith and loving service to others is oblivious to the concepts of self-glorification and personal ambition. For the Christian disciple who has an empty vessel open to God for service, the Holy Spirit can prepare ahead of time people in need of ministry and bring them across our path for salvation, healing, deliverance, or encouragement. This is the formula that produces eternally beneficial results.

God knows our spiritual capacity. God knows the needs of people in our immediate, physical vicinity. The Holy Spirit can bring the two together. Our part is to be "prayed up," live the quality of life that can produce the words of Life when called upon, to be willing and open to be used by God, and to give God the credit and the glory when we see positive results. This approach works for the most average of Christian disciples and for the greatest apostles like Philip, John, Paul, and Peter.

The way to greater power and anointing under the Holy Spirit, like that displayed in the lives of the first century apostles and disciples, is through the humility illustrated by Jesus when he placed the child in the midst of the apostles. The way to real spiritual power is not through succumbing to the temptation to become "somebody" in the Christian world, thereby mimicking what occurs in the conventional outside world. The spirit and attitude of the Christian is supposed to be the opposite of the spirit of this world. The most prepared person for God's use is not "full" of themselves, but "empty" of themselves. The greatest among us are supposed to be the least in terms of haughtiness and worldly pride. The chiefest is supposed to be servant of all. The person who is truly walking in the Spirit is devoid of self-awareness and self-recognition.

Even experienced, mature, and savvy Christians walk a fine line in this area. As God transforms us into sons and daughters of light, we always have to recognize our need for God. The proud and arrogant cannot do this. That is why the process of salvation begins with humility and repentance, and continues that way as long as we draw breath on this earth.

We Are Emissaries of the King

It might be well to pause for a moment of reflection here. The apostles were in the inner circle of being disciples of *the Creator of the Universe, the eternal Word of God.* Yet *none* of these men showed signs in their subsequent early church ministries of trying to cash-in on their relationship with Jesus Christ to make something of themselves. The same can be said of the prophets in the Old Testament. The price-tag of being in the confidence of the Almighty God is having the high character trait of selflessness, of being willing to be trustworthy and dependable *agents* of the king...of not seeking our own interests.

Imagine the privilege and responsibility of being called to be even a "minor" prophet in the Old Testament by God Himself...to be trusted with God's message and mission to take to other people. This requires the highest character in conformity to Jesus Christ through the Holy Spirit. Serving God the

Father, through Jesus Christ, in the power of the Holy Spirit, is traveling in the highest company. To aspire to this requires the most sober humility in a human being. Being entrusted to take God's redemptive message of life out into a broken world is a serious endeavor, allowing no room for self-adulation or personal acclaim. This is the lesson in placing a small, innocent child in the midst of the disciples, as an example of the correct selfless spirit in serving God faithfully in any capacity.

People will try to push people up in Christendom (John 6:15). If I am "somebody" this does absolutely nothing for you. Only if Jesus is somebody important in our lives does something happen for the good. The right approach is to lift up Jesus, not people. Being a selfless servant of God is what produces eternally beneficial results.

Every Christian should be on guard and aware of spiritual pride. In everything we do, but especially in our Christian service, we should remember the insightfully classic words of the Greek Gentiles seeking an audience with Jesus by approaching Philip during the Passover feast in Jerusalem: "Sir, we would see Jesus" (John 12:21). As professing Christians, we should always be pointing people's vision toward Jesus and away from ourselves.

Chapter Five

The Spiritual Vision of John the Baptist

If ye, then, be risen with Christ, seek those things which are above, where Christ sitteth on the right hand of God. Set your affection on things above, not on things on the earth. For ye are dead, and your life is hidden with Christ in God.
Colossians 3:1-3

John the Baptist, through the Holy Spirit, was able to spiritually see the multitudes of people in Israel who needed repentance, salvation, and reform. When John captures God's love-filled vision of repentance for Israel, and begins to preach the message that God gave him in the wilderness, the New Testament says: "Then went out to him Jerusalem, and all Judea, and all the region round about the Jordan" (Matthew 3:5).

Paul, in the midst of his evangelical ministry to the Mediterranean world, says that God has set forth the apostles as being last (1 Corinthians 4:9). Only from the low vantage point of humility can the leaders of the early Christian church spiritually see the field of lost people ready for repentance and harvesting into the kingdom of God. A large number of people were ready to turn to God in first century Israel and in the Greco-Roman Mediterranean world, but the Pharisees, scribes, and other religious leaders in Jerusalem were unable to see, much less minister to this need. Self-centeredness and self-importance blocks our spiritual vision of the needs of other people.

The Pharisees and scribes unwittingly revealed their true character by criticizing Jesus for associating with damaged, needy, and broken people, when they ask the disciples: "Why eateth your Master with publicans and sinners?" (Matthew 9:11). Jesus said that He came to "seek and to save that which was lost" (Luke 19:10). The narrowly exclusive outreach of the Pharisees and scribes does not include the outcasts and undesirables of society, because the Pharisees are sitting in self-righteous pride, high atop the thrones of their lives.

Lucifer certainly has no intention of seeking and saving the lost sheep of Israel. Jesus says of the Pharisees and scribes, at the height of their power and influence, and while the Temple in Jerusalem is fully functioning as a religious institution, that these men are as the blind leading the blind (Matthew 15:14). The Pharisees and scribes are spiritually blind because they cannot see

30

the multitudes of people in Israel, ready and willing to come to John, hear his message at the river Jordan, and to confess their sins and be water baptized.

The Pharisees and scribes are blind because they cannot see, from their high perch atop the thrones of their hearts, those people in Israel who are spiritually sick and in need of God the Great Physician (Matthew 9:12). John the Baptist, Jesus, and the early church Christians in Jerusalem have to do the work that the Pharisees and scribes were supposed to be doing, but were not, because it takes a life genuinely lived according to the cross of Christ to be able to spiritually see, empathize with, and commit ourselves to meeting the needs of lost and broken people.

The Pharisees and chief priests revealed their true heart condition when they said: "If we let him thus alone, all men will believe on him; and the Romans shall come and take away both our place and nation" (John 11:48). If we are called, if we are prepared for ministry through the experience of the cross, if we have God's vision of the needs of the lost in this world…then *no one* can take away our place except by the express will of God Almighty (1 Peter 3:13). By saying that the Romans can come and take away their place, these religious leaders are unknowingly admitting that their worldly-based authority does not derive from a divine, unshakable godly calling to minister to the lost people of this world.

Even though multitudes of people were ready to come to the Jordan River to repent and be baptized, God could not enlist the Pharisees and scribes to this great work, because they could not even see the need. If Christians today want to go forth into their Christian ministries with their spiritual eyes fully open to be able to see the needs of others, the road of preparation that leads there is the lowly way of the cross.

One of the basic lessons of the life of John the Baptist that applies to all Christians is that the godly life may not always appear to be successful, at times, in the eyes of the world. No one had any idea what John was doing, quietly allowing God to prepare him in the desert for his spectacular upcoming ministry. No one in Canaan knew at the time Abraham showed up that the future "father of faith" had arrived. Joseph appears to be a complete failure in Potiphar's house and in Pharaoh's prison.

Conventional wisdom would say that Moses was committing suicide by going to Egypt and demanding from Pharaoh that he let the children of Israel go.

As King Saul is pursuing David on several occasions to kill him, David is only separated from him by a hilltop. Considering the potential that David showed at the beginning of his career, in slaying Goliath and in his early military victories against the Philistines, some people at the time might conclude that David in his middle to late twenties had become a huge disappointment.

Everything about Jesus…what He says, teaches, and does is unconventional. When we accept Jesus into our lives, we become new people with improved characters and attitudes, but we also have a new faith in Christ that can bring the unconventional, supernatural aspect of Jesus into our own set of life events and circumstances.

Christians who want to follow God's plan for their lives must confront and overcome the negative pull of worldly conventional thinking. God is not for or against wealth or poverty, nor is He for or against the appearance of success or failure. These things are totally beside the point in a biblical journey of faith applied to our lives. God is not assisted by wealth and success or limited by poverty and the appearance of failure. We are supposed to surrender all to Jesus right where we find ourselves, to listen for His voice to become a light and a blessing to ourselves and to those around us, and to be open and accessible to God's leading wherever that takes us. This is one of the lessons we can learn from the enormously powerful and world-shaking ministry of John the Baptist.

God knows that some people have the God-given abilities to become an outward success in this world. God knows how to reach these types of people and call them by His Spirit to respond to His love, and to surrender their lives to His plans and purposes. God also knows how to reach people who have gifts and talents that are not likely to produce great worldly acclaim or wealth, and to craft lives for them that are more fulfilling and meaningful than anything they could have imagined for themselves. If faith in God is described in the Bible as comparable to fine gold (1 Peter 1:7), then even the most average Christian can aspire to and experience a world-class life following Jesus Christ.

Chapter Six

Desperation Can Push Us into Reliance upon God

"My brethren, count it all joy when ye fall into various trials, Knowing this, that the trying of your faith worketh patience. But let patience have her perfect work, that ye may be perfect and entire, lacking nothing."   James 1:2-4

In the Gospels and in The Acts of the New Testament there are many examples of human crisis, desperation, and need. Luke 8:22 through 8:56 presents four such examples of people who have reached the point of desperation in their lives, who turn to Jesus for help. They were the disciples in jeopardy in the storm at sea, the man who had the legion of demons cast out, the woman who touched the border of Jesus' garment, and Jairus the ruler of a synagogue.

In Luke 8:22-25, the disciples and Jesus are in a boat crossing a lake, when a strong wind creates a storm dangerous enough to place their lives at risk. But Jesus fell asleep at the beginning of their journey across the lake and is still asleep as water from the waves are coming into and filling up the boat. The disciples wake up Jesus, and excitedly say to Him "Master, master, we perish." Jesus rebukes the wind and the waves, and there was calm where moments before there was a perilous storm. Luke 8:25 reads "And he said unto them, Where is your faith? And they, being afraid, marveled, saying one to another, What manner of man is this! For he commandeth even the winds and water, and they obey him."

Because this story is so brief, and the happy ending comes so quickly, it is easy to gloss over the serious import of this story. On board this boat were probably most of the apostles, although none of them are mentioned specifically by name. John was probably on board, who wrote the fourth gospel, three letters to the churches, and the book of The Revelation. Peter was probably on board, who by tradition provided the information for the writing of the gospel of Mark, wrote two letters to the churches, and figures prominently in the book of Acts and in the first century church. Matthew was probably also on board the floundering boat, who wrote the first gospel. A good portion of the entire New Testament, not to mention Jesus Himself, was riding in that boat on the lake. For Peter and Andrew, and James and John, who were all fishermen by trade, to awaken Jesus and to say they were on the verge of perishing, meant that the storm was serious. To the apostles the moment was desperate.

The solution that Jesus brings to this otherwise life and death situation is not on the list of normal responses to save a boat that is floundering at sea. We do not know what the apostles had in mind for Jesus to do during this crisis, but it probably fell somewhere within the realm of solid advice on how to reach land while working together as a team bailing water out of the boat. The idea that Jesus would stand up in the boat and rebuke the wind and the waves to produce an almost instant calm was a solution to the problem that was way above and beyond the possible options the apostles might have possibly imagined.

The story of the man who had the legion of demons cast out can certainly be described as desperate. He lived as a naked madman amongst rocks and caves, and when the demons were cast out of him by Jesus they entered into a herd of swine that ran headlong over a cliff into the sea and drowned. This situation is so far beyond human ability to resolve in terms of counseling or psychology, that even today we must marvel at the outcome of this man sitting at the feet of Jesus, clothed, and in his right mind. This story seems commonplace for Jesus, only because it is mixed in among so many other miracles, healings, and deliverances Jesus performed.

The woman who was healed by touching the border of Jesus' garment had an issue of blood for twelve years, and had spent all of her finances on physicians without being cured. She was desperate to the point of thinking within herself that, although she could not gain personal access to Jesus amongst all of the people who crowded around Him, if she could just reach out and touch His garment as He walked by she might be healed. In this brief but wonderful story, Jesus is the last hope for this woman.

Jairus, the ruler of a synagogue, reaches the point of desperation on account of the deadly illness of his twelve year old daughter, his only child. Jairus falls at the feet of Jesus, asking Him to come to his house and heal his daughter. The situation becomes hopeless when the house servant arrives to tell Jairus that his daughter has died. But Jairus has already committed himself to include Jesus in his personal crisis, and Jesus does not abandon the situation. Jesus has the power to resolve this impossible problem, even to the point of being able to bring a young woman back from the dead.

In every situation in the New Testament, when anyone approaches Jesus in faith with a need or a request, no matter how desperate or seemingly impossible, Jesus always succeeds. When people approached Jesus in faith, I can think of no example where Jesus was not able to heal an illness, provide for a need, or solve a problem. Only three occasions come to mind where Jesus actually failed in the New Testament. Because of people's unbelief, Jesus was not able to perform many miracles in His hometown of Nazareth (Mark 6:5-6). Because of people's unbelief, Jesus was not able to persuade and win over the majority of the Pharisees, scribes, and teachers of the Law, and was eventually crucified through their instigation. Because of people's unbelief, the city of Jerusalem was not able to receive the blessings and protection that God had in mind for it and suffered instead the wrath of the Roman Empire in A.D. 70 as the Roman general Titus destroyed the city.

The only time that God ever "fails," is when people or nations push Him away. In every situation where there is some measure of faith involved, Jesus is able to save a wedding feast by turning water into wine, heal lepers, restore sight to the blind, raise the dead, feed thousands of people in a desert, calm a storm at sea, and walk harmlessly through a crowd of people intent upon throwing Him off a cliff. In these situations and circumstances, Jesus never fails.

When we combine the fact that God never fails, and the concept as presented in this book that the plans of God for people maneuver them to a point of having to rely solely upon Him, above and beyond their own personal gifts and talents, we get a better picture of the direction the Christian life is supposed to be going. This is why so many verses, stories, and parables in the Bible talk about placing our faith and trust in God as opposed to self-reliance (Isaiah 53:6; Proverbs 3:5-6). The idea that God is still in control, even in situations and circumstances that are difficult is sometimes portrayed in the Bible just below the surface of a particular story. Other times, this idea is clearly expressed.

For example, when Abraham receives his calling from God to leave the town of Haran and travel to the promised land of Canaan, it is implied in this story that he must thereby leave behind all of his Haran-based plans, designs, and schemes that are now displaced by the new Canaan-based plan of God for him. Not only is Abraham heading off into new territory geographically, but also into new territory spiritually. What lies just below the surface in this story is that once Abraham commits to following God into this new unconventional life-plan, Abraham becomes completely and totally dependent upon God to bring about the successful completion of God's promise to him. Because Abraham does believe God, and because God never fails, God's promise to Abraham does eventually come true. But not before God is able to fashion Abraham, through a series of well-planned and orchestrated events, into the type of person that can rightly be called the "father of faith."

1 Peter 4:12 reads "Beloved, think it not strange concerning the fiery trial that is to test you, as though some strange thing happened unto you." This verse and many similar verses in the Bible expressly say that periods in our Christian lives will have situations and circumstances that are above and beyond our ability to handle. If we can look back upon, or are currently in situations that require us to cry out to God "save me, I perish," then we are learning lessons of faith and trust in God that match the experiences of people of faith in the Bible who reached similar points of desperation. We are being crafted into overcomers who can face any and all of life's challenges with patient confidence through our personal relationship with a trustworthy and faithful God.

Chapter Seven

The Event of the Cross

All we like sheep have gone astray; we have turned every one to his own way, and the Lord hath laid on Him the iniquity of us all.   Isaiah 53:6

When Jesus Christ confronted the religious leaders in Jerusalem, as recorded in the four gospels, at that time the Pharisees, Sadducees, lawyers, and scribes were in possession of the worldly political seat of power. They had the power to influence the opinion of the populace against Jesus, to throw out of the synagogue anyone who professed belief in Jesus, to slander His person, to marginalize His teachings, and eventually have Jesus crucified by the Romans as a political and societal enemy of the state (John 19:12). A small, exclusive club of spiritually blind and worldly self-centered men was in political control in Jerusalem during the ministry of Jesus.

Yet during this entire period, God is able to engineer and accomplish all of His plans and designs for the salvation of mankind, which He meticulously laid-out ahead of time in the Old Testament messianic prophecies and "types" of Christ hundreds of years earlier. This is an important observation as we approach the last days. God worked His complete agenda for mankind's salvation within and through the political plans and schemes of evil men during the same time period these men thought they had the upper hand and were in control of events. This gives us a foreglimpse of the scenario that may repeat itself again in the upcoming end-times.

An argument can be made that it is the violently lethal differences of opinion that form the basis for the martyrdom of Jesus of Nazareth as the Lamb of God sacrifice for our sins. It is the heat of the conflict created within God's resolution of the difference between right and wrong, and truth and error, which surprisingly generates the outcome of Christ's sacrifice on the cross as the foundation of our salvation. That God is creatively brilliant enough to mint a heavenly coin of salvation, having the exposure of error and falsehood on one side of the coin, and redemption from sin through the atonement of Christ on the cross and resurrection from the dead on the other side of the coin, is remarkable beyond all human reckoning. This plainly tells us that God can move through real-life events and circumstances having the darkest outward appearance of adversity and opposition, to accomplish His plans with creative imagination and foresight to rival the best of modern fictional suspense novelists.

The religious leaders in Jerusalem had the political power, but God had control of all of the events, situations, and circumstances to achieve the outcome He wanted. This is one of the most important revelations in the Bible, which is understood and acknowledged on a surface level in all of Christendom, yet is seldom explored very deeply. *Whoever can supernaturally shape events controls everything.*

There is only one divine, all-powerful God in all of existence. This is one of the things Jesus is trying to tell us about our choices, and the direction of our lives, in The Sermon on the Mount. This is one of the foundations of faith in Jesus Christ. This is why Christians walking in the Spirit surrender all to Jesus. This is why people of faith in the Bible, in the midst of their calling, give up control of events to God. God is so intelligent and resourceful that He can even take the evil actions of worldly people and turn them into good outcomes.

The action of crucifying the Son of God cannot get any more darkly evil, yet God turned it into the greatest blessing for good for all eternity. If the worst that evil can do,

unjustly condemning and executing Jesus the Son of God, ends up actually providing the means for the best outcome in human history...the salvation and deliverance of mankind from sin...then evil does not stand a chance when people choose God. God is so intelligent and resourceful that He can take the very ammunition that evil shoots at spiritual righteousness, and turn it back around upon itself.

Although the human side of Jesus did not look forward joyfully toward the physical agony of the cross, Jesus was not afraid of evil. Jesus knew that God the Father would take the deadly attack of evil upon Himself, as symbolized in the cross, turning this around into eternal salvation for mankind. When we are safely "in Christ" through faith, and because "all things work together for good for them that love God, to them who are the called according to his purpose" (Romans 8:28), we do not have to be afraid of the appearance of evil coming against us in the situations and circumstances of life. This includes the upcoming end-times.

The point of this chapter is to illustrate that it was the *event* of the cross of Christ, spread out in time over many finely detailed circumstances, which not only divided spiritual light from darkness, but at the same time demonstrated God's complete mastery over the affairs of men. It did not matter that the religious leaders in Jerusalem had the political and social power. God's use of situations and circumstances is on a level that is way above the temporal political powers on earth.

The messianic prophecies and types of Christ in the Old Testament that apply to the cross are too numerous to exhaustively cover in this chapter. Briefly, Abraham says to Isaac: "My son, God will provide himself a lamb for a burnt offering" (Genesis 22:8). The blood of the Passover lamb was applied to the two sides and upper door lintel of the house, representing the human heart (Exodus 12:1-28). The rock, which Moses struck once with his rod in Horeb to produce water is a type of Christ (Exodus 17:5-6; John 4:14). The bronze serpent on a pole is a preview of the cross (Numbers 21:8-9; John 3:14). Psalms 22:16 says: "they pierced my hands and my feet." Psalms 22:17 foretells that the Romans did not break the legs of Jesus on the cross to hasten His death before sunset preceding the Sabbath, because He was already dead. Psalms 22:18 says: "They part my garments among them, and cast lots upon my vesture." The 53rd chapter of Isaiah says that Christ will be despised and rejected of men (53:3), wounded for our transgressions (53:5), open not his mouth in his own defense (53:7), make his grave with the rich (53:9), and be executed alongside transgressors (53:12).

Within the hostile environment that Jesus operated throughout much of His ministry (John 7:1), but especially during His final week in Jerusalem (John 7:32; John 8:59; John 10:31), how is it that God the Father can orchestrate the timing of the crucifixion down to the precise day of the Passover, and the traditional hour of the day the Passover lamb is killed? Jesus is betrayed by Judas after the Last Supper on Thursday evening, is hastily tried at the house of Caiaphas very late on Thursday night and early Friday morning, the sentence of death is ratified by the Sanhedrin at daybreak on Friday, the prisoner is placed before Pilate for formal sentencing early Friday morning, and Jesus is hanging on the cross around 9:00 in the morning of Friday the Passover. Jesus dies around 3:00 or 4:00 that afternoon, the time that the Passover lambs are traditionally killed.

God the Father steps on the accelerator pedal to speed up events before and during that last week, first by creating a sense of urgency on the part of the

39

religious leaders, through Jesus raising Lazarus from the dead, and His triumphal entrance into Jerusalem. God then alternately taps with His foot on the brakes and then touches the accelerator pedal again lightly through the indecisiveness of the religious leaders on the one hand and the information that Judas provides on the other. This achieves just the right velocity to get Jesus crucified within the narrow time window between sundown Thursday and sundown Friday, according to all of the ancient Old Testament prophecies on the very day of the Passover.

This is an incredibly difficult thing to orchestrate over the span of a three-and-one-half year long ministry, when the life of Jesus was in danger on several occasions, starting at the beginning of His ministry in His own hometown of Nazareth (Luke 4:29). This achievement is even more remarkable considering that the Pharisees, scribes, and religious leaders in Jerusalem were not prophets of God being led by His Spirit, but deadly adversaries in opposition to the ways of God. God was using them for His purposes without their knowledge or awareness of this fact.

The Pharisees, Sadducees, and scribes could have arrested Jesus on any night of that final week on His way back from Jerusalem to the Mount of Olives (Luke 21:37). They could have arrested Him any morning of that week on His way to teach in the Temple. They did not need Judas to tell them the whereabouts of Jesus.[2] His movements were so well known that "the people came early in the morning to him in the temple, to hear him" (Luke 21:38). A crowd of people was awaiting Him alongside the road during His triumphal entrance into the city (John 12:12). The gospels tell us that the religious leaders did fear the reaction of the people should they make a move against Jesus (Mark 12:12; Luke 19:47-48; Luke 20:6). That was certainly a restraining element in their calculations. But the religious leaders also feared Jesus Himself. Jesus was an unknown quantity. They were not even sure if it was possible to arrest Him (John 7:30; John 7:45-46; John 8:20; John 8:59; John 10:39). They knew they wanted to eliminate Him, they just did not know exactly when and how they would do it. God Himself provided the answer.

It took a member of the inner group of His closest disciples, Judas Iscariot, to change allegiance from Jesus over to the religious leaders, to become

---

[2] Frank Morison, Who Moved the Stone (Downers Grove, Illinois: InterVarsity Press) 30-42. The reconstructions of the events of the final week in Jerusalem described in this chapter, are taken from this insightful book.

the means of propulsion that God used to govern and adjust the speed of the events that led to the midnight trial and the Passover crucifixion. Being one of the twelve apostles, Judas naturally heard Jesus speaking to the group as they approached Jerusalem that final week, preparing them beforehand for His upcoming death and resurrection (Matthew 20:17-19; Mark 10:32-34; Luke 18:31-34).

The value of Judas' information that week to the religious rulers was not so much the whereabouts of Jesus, which many people seemed to know about, but the fact that someone in His inner circle was telling them that Jesus was speaking mysteriously and unexplainably about His upcoming death. That was the unexpected and welcome information that was worth thirty pieces of silver from Caiaphas the High Priest and the other rulers, not just where Jesus was at any particular moment.

Luke 18:34 tells us that the twelve apostles did not understand what Jesus meant when He told them, as they journeyed toward Jerusalem, that He would be put to death and rise the third day. Even though Judas, like the other eleven apostles, would not have understood these words of Jesus, yet he could still pass along this critical information word-for-word to the religious leaders, having heard them first-hand from Jesus.

Jesus knew that Judas would betray Him (John 6:64; John 6:70-71; John 13:11). There seems to be a sort of understanding between Jesus and Judas that Jesus would be waiting in the Garden of Gethsemane that Thursday night, when Jesus says to Judas: "What thou doest, do quickly" (John 13:27). It is this startling, confirming information, accurately perceived by Judas during the Last Supper, and hurriedly communicated by him to the rulers, that sets in motion the final decision by Caiaphas the High Priest to go forward with the destruction of Jesus (Matthew 26:3-5).

But all of the proper proceedings must now be started and consummated by sundown the following day, before the start of the Sabbath. Criminals executed by crucifixion could not be left dead on their crosses after sunset at the start of the Friday night Sabbath. That is why the legs of the two thieves crucified next to Jesus were broken that afternoon, to facilitate their death and removal that same afternoon. Add to this the complication that the Passover was the first day of the week-long Feast of Unleavened Bread. If Jesus could not be tried, executed, and disposed of that Friday, he would have had to be held over under their custody until after the festival week. Any problem or glitch in the proceedings that did not result in a conviction and a crucifixion the following day, could have unforeseen and very unpleasant consequences regarding the reaction of the people, for these rulers. The thing had to be carried out to its conclusion quickly, before public sentiment could galvanize one way or the other.

This explains why the party of Jesus lingers in the Garden of Gethsemane much later than usual, causing the disciples to fall asleep. This is why Caiaphas himself probably went to Pilate late Thursday night (a reasonable inference, though not recorded in scripture) to get Pilate's pre-arranged consent for the course of action the Jewish leaders proposed to take the following day. This is why Pilate's wife, becoming aware of the subject nature of the unusual late night visit of Caiaphas to speak with her husband, had bad dreams that very night about Jesus (Matthew 27:19), and sent a note forewarning Pilate at daybreak the next morning. This is why Pilate seems to go back on his agreement with Caiaphas from the night before, to summarily go along with the Jew's death sentence for Jesus, and instead attempts first to set Jesus free. This greatly upsets the already committed Jewish leaders (John 18:30). Pilate then proceeds to wash his hands of the whole affair (Matthew 27:24).

This is why Judas knows exactly where to take the hastily assembled group of armed men carrying lanterns and torches, when Jesus and the apostles should otherwise normally be asleep at that late hour elsewhere at the Mount of Olives. This is why Jesus waits and stays where He is, even though He can probably see the procession of lanterns and torches a long way off as the crowd approaches (Matthew 26:46). Jesus also knows that Judas is heading for the Garden of Gethsemane.

The timing of the final betrayal of Jesus by Judas on Thursday night (the Passover starts at sundown on Thursday), and the constraint of having to consummate everything by sundown the following day, the start of the Sabbath, effectively narrows the crucifixion of Jesus Christ the "Lamb slain from the foundation of the world" (Revelation 13:8) to the day of the Passover. The religious rulers thought they were in control, but God set up all of these events to lead to the outcome He had planned long ago (1 Corinthians 2:8).

What Does This Mean for Christians Today?

When modern-day Christians read this account of how much precise planning and effort was put in by God to accomplish something as important as the crucifixion of His Son Jesus, the natural question might be asked would God care that much about me to put in the same quality and amount of thought, planning, and care into the situations and circumstances of my life? From the biblical accounts in the four gospels of the cross and the resurrection, we see what God is capable of doing. But if I yield and surrender my life to God, like Jesus did, can I count on God being able and willing to divide truth from error in my life, and to arrange events large and small to produce good for myself and others on some scale to match the brilliance we see in the life of Jesus? Will God write a script for me with as much care and precision like He did with the fine-tuned events surrounding the cross and the resurrection?

The answer to this fundamental question of the Christian life is already previewed within the account of the events of the cross itself. Already contained within the intricately planned and executed events of the cross is a pattern in action of God's outreach to mankind and to each individual person. The cross and the resurrection were not for the sake of Jesus. They were for us. The cross is God's gift of love to mankind to reconcile us back to Himself. It shouts with sublime passion "I love you enough to take upon myself the inescapable penalty for sin."

In the well-crafted details of Jesus experiencing the events of the cross and the resurrection, we see God's demonstrated intention and desire to work for and within every person who chooses Him this same imaginative control of life's events for our benefit. God lovingly participates in the details of our lives, always through the pattern of the cross and the resurrection. This is part of the overall program and agenda of being re-connected to God, which starts with the cross.

If we are "in Christ," like Jesus and the Father are one, we have the same God carefully orchestrating events in our lives as well (John 17:23). This begins with the unique and different set of life circumstances which brings each of us to a salvation quality, born-again faith. This is why the Holy Spirit lives within the born-again Christian, to lead us into all truth, through experiences composed and guided just for us by God Himself (John 14:16-17). This is a part of the good news of the gospel...that God has imaginative solutions to the individual challenges of our lives through Jesus Christ, starting with the solution of the cross to the human problem of sin and finishing with a meaningful and purposeful walk of faith in service to God.

43

The Pharisees, Sadducees, scribes, and lawyers in Jerusalem remained unchanged all the way up to 70 A.D. They were still erroneously looking for their worldly political and military style messiah who would free them from Rome and establish economic and political prosperity. They pushed God away during the inspired ministry of John the Baptist. They rejected and crucified Jesus the Christ. They persecuted the early Christian church. They were eventually crushed by the Roman army under Titus in 70 A.D., who demolished their city Jerusalem and scattered the Jews throughout the Middle East, Northern Africa, and Europe for the next 1900 years.

The essence of sin says to God: "Who are you to tell me what to do or how to live my life," and "why should I go by your standards instead of my own?" These questions are difficult to answer back using words only. They require a practical demonstration of the pros and cons through actual life experience. They require a test where success and failure are real possibilities. That is one of the reasons why this current world exists. The cross of Christ is the key, pivotal demonstration of the answer. A beneficent God says: "I have your best interests at heart...my *actions* on the cross for you prove this...follow me...I have been around a long time...I know what I am doing." People of faith accept the invitation, believe, and follow. Rebellious people who are carnally minded and living in the flesh, like the example of the first century Pharisees, Sadducees, and scribes, say: "No, we will live by our own wisdom and volition."

God has already laid-out in detail the events of the end-times. They are all there in verses scattered throughout the Old Testament, in the four gospels, in the book of Acts, in the letters of the apostles to the churches, and in the book of Revelation. Additional detailed information will be revealed some day through the dreams, visions, and prophesies described in Joel 2:28-29. Just like the ministries of John the Baptist and Jesus, these end-times events are already scripted-out and have a definite starting time in the near future. As with the events leading up to the cross, God's ingenious plans and designs will be interwoven into the fabric of the end-times political events, working His will and exposing truth versus error for one last emphatic time in human history.

Chapter Eight

Becoming Last for Jesus, in the End-Times

For I think that God hath set forth us, the apostles, last.   1 Corinthians 4:9

As Paul traveled the first century Mediterranean world as a missionary evangelist, his first-rate rabbinical education under Gamaliel in Jerusalem served him well. As he and Barnabas or Silas entered a synagogue in a new city, Paul was probably in every case better educated and more knowledgeable about Old Testament scripture than the local rabbi of that synagogue. This element in Paul's background of the highest scholarly qualifications removed from consideration any attack based upon lack of education, on the credibility of Paul's message that Jesus Christ is the Messiah. Within the unique context of Paul's calling and mission to the Jews and Gentiles of the larger Mediterranean world, the above-reproach credentials of Paul's rabbinical training and education were mandatory and invaluable.

Yet when Paul meets Jesus Christ on the road to Damascus, and begins his career of preaching that the cross and the resurrection proved that Jesus of Nazareth was the Messiah, Paul suffers the loss of the prestige and honor that his formal education would normally have afforded him in the Jewish culture. Paul entered into the rejection that Jesus referred to in Matthew 10:24-25: "If they have called the master of the house Beelzebub, how much more shall they call them of his household?" In Paul's own words in Philippians 3:4-10, Paul says that he has "suffered the loss of all things." In Corinthians 1:23, Paul says: "But we preach Christ crucified, unto the Jews a stumbling block, and unto the Gentiles foolishness."

Earlier in 1 Corinthians 1:18, Paul says: "For the preaching of the cross is to them that perish foolishness." In 1 Corinthians 4:9-16, as quoted above, Paul says that God has set forth the apostles as last, as a spectacle to the world, as fools, weak, despised, naked, hungry, buffeted, reviled, persecuted, defamed, and as the filth and offscouring of the world. Yet Paul actually concludes this section of scriptures by saying in the 16th verse, to be followers of him in this regard, as being the normal, expected outcome of committed, uncompromising discipleship.

45

While speaking to Ananias in a vision, Jesus says about Paul: "For I will show him how great things he must suffer for my names sake" (Acts 9:16). Paul narrowly escapes the threat of death in Damascus (Acts 9:23-25), again escapes the threat of death in Jerusalem (Acts 9:29-30), is expelled out of a city (Acts 13:50), is stoned (Acts 14:19), is beaten and jailed (Acts 16:23), is the cause of a riot (Acts 17:5), is accused before Gallio in Achaia (Acts 18:12), is the cause of another riot in Ephesus (Acts 19:23-41). Paul is beaten by the mob in Jerusalem (Acts 21:32), nearly "pulled in pieces" by the Pharisees and Sadducees in the Sanhedrin (Acts 23:10), is in danger of forty men sworn to kill him (Acts 23:12), is imprisoned for purely political reasons (Acts 24:27), and is shipwrecked in a perilous sea as a prisoner on his way to a trial before Caesar in Rome (Acts 27:39-44).

If the Apostle Paul is one of our best examples of the true Christian, and if this joint-venture type journey-of-faith is the pathway *that God chose* for Paul to become a Holy Spirit validated writer of some of the divinely inspired New Testament, then Paul's experiences instruct us as to one of the singular truths of all eternity. This truth is that the power and wisdom of God working in our lives invariably leads to Holy Spirit manufactured humility. The greatest athlete, the most talented movie actor, and most brilliant scientist, are at their best when they do not have to brag about or tout themselves.

The perfect, divine example of this is Jesus Christ, who contrary to conventional wisdom, "made himself of no reputation" and "took upon him the form of a servant" and "humbled himself and became obedient unto death, even the death of the cross" (Philippians 2:7-8). When engineered by the Holy Spirit working in our lives, the actualization of our unique God-given talents blended with some measure of divine humility, is a miraculous, supernatural product that is manufactured within us through the series of events that make up a biblical quality journey of faith.

This is part of what the lives of Paul and the other great men and women of faith in the Bible is telling us. It is the supernatural participation of God that makes these biblical life stories different, extraordinary, and exceptional compared to conventional human life stories. The lives of the biblical characters are different because God is different…His ways are higher than our ways (Isaiah 55:9).

In a worldly conventional sense, how does a person apply for the job opening of governor of Egypt, with a resume that is as weak on its surface as

46

Joseph's? Joseph was merely a head-servant in Potiphar's house, and merely a helper of the keeper of the king's prison where Joseph himself was a prisoner. But in reality Joseph truly is qualified for leadership at the highest management level to become governor of Egypt, through God's imaginatively conceived training regime. *Yet only God knows this.*

On paper, in a worldly conventional context there is absolutely no way whatsoever that Joseph would ever, even momentarily, be considered for such a powerful and prestigious position. Joseph is not even Egyptian. Yet God can compose, orchestrate, and bring to pass the incredible events that shape the story of Joseph's life. This enormous leap from Pharaoh's prison to becoming the governor of Egypt is an example of the supernatural participation of God in our lives. *Worldly conventional wisdom and God's supernatural approach do not mix, but are on the extreme opposite ends of the scale of the imaginable and the possible.*

Similarly, in a worldly conventional sense, how does a person who is starting at the very bottom like the 17-year old David, follow God's supernatural lead to take them all the way up to the height of personal achievement in becoming the king of Israel? This is a one-in-a-million long-shot for the youngest son in a large family of older brothers, whose only life experience, on paper, is as a shepherd and musician (1 Samuel 16:18). No one outside of David's immediate family even knows that God sent the prophet Samuel to seek out and anoint among the sons of Jesse a future king for Israel.

But David does show such great early potential in killing Goliath, and defeating the Philistines in several battles that King Saul eventually realizes that David will someday supplant his own son Jonathan for the throne of Israel. Yet events on the road to becoming king are so daunting and challenging, much like Paul's numerous challenges centuries later as a missionary evangelist that David can write in Psalm twenty-three about God's supernatural protective presence as David walks through the valley of the very shadow of death.

Only God can craft such an incredibly unconventional journey to the throne of Israel, combining commendable character-building lessons along the way such as faith, honor, patience, determination, humility, and courage that are in such contrast to the worldly approaches of graft, corruption, nepotism, favoritism, political intrigue, and outright military rebellion to obtain a kingship, so typical in secular history.

Again, from a worldly conventional sense, how does a person apply for the narrowly specific job opening of missionary evangelist to the Greco-Roman world of the first century, with Paul's extremely contrary past history? Paul as Saul the Pharisee was the deadliest enemy of the early church. On paper, Paul is an absolute disaster as a future Christian evangelist, before the time of his turn-around conversion at Damascus. Paul is the last person on the planet that conventional wisdom would consider and single-out as a viable candidate to preach the message to the first century world that Jesus of Nazareth is our way to God. Only Almighty God can craft the brilliantly creative character journey that spans the wide gulf from Saul the persecutor to about twenty-five years later as Paul the beloved apostle of Romans chapter sixteen.

The events and circumstances of a truly godly, biblical-quality life are not things we can simply manufacture ourselves. This is what makes the God of the Bible and the unique storylines of the lives of the people of faith in the Bible, different from anyone or anything else in human experience. A biblical life with God is a journey into the unconventional. The lives of Joseph and David could have been much different and much easier...they could have been ordinary. But then the lives of Joseph and David would not have been biblical. What makes their lives special and a divinely crafted pattern-for-faith recorded in the Bible, is this supernatural overlay of the plans and will of God on top of what otherwise would be impossible circumstances and conditions.

Only God can set up the unconventional situations and circumstances that lead us to the cross, and to the critical decision to abandon our own self-sovereignty and surrender our way to God's better and higher knowledge. Either God is God, knows best, and has the power to intervene supernaturally for our benefit, or He is not.

God knows that He can give to Pharaoh a puzzling dream that will initiate the cascade of events that will result in Joseph becoming governor of all Egypt. God knows how to take a rough-cut diamond like David and craft him into a king. As modern-day Christians, we cannot discover the eternally valid lesson of the faithfulness of God without stepping out into the risk of an adventure of faith following God wherever He leads.

The supernatural power of God for character transformation and Christian service comes with the prerequisite of divine love and genuine humility, purchased through a God-composed and guided measure of hardship within our journey of faith. This is one element that sets the godly biblical life

48

uniquely apart. As Christians, we are at our finest and best when our characters exhibit the divine quality of self-effacing, vaunteth-not-itself, servant-like humility exemplified in biblical characters like Joseph, Moses, David, Paul, Peter, and of course Jesus Christ.

This is the creative dilemma and challenge for God. How does God manufacture a person like Joseph, with the capacity to rule Egypt as governor, yet with the independent virtue to reject through his own free-will choice, the destructive pride of an Absalom corrupted by self-centered, self-adoration. How does God create a person having the innate abilities of a Joseph, who can learn through carefully guided yet difficult experience, to emulate the near-divine, high level of character to be able to forgive out of his own free-will the earlier trespasses of his brothers, through unselfish and bitterness-free grace? How does God create people close enough in quality to Himself in order to be able to enjoy a meaningful relationship with, like an Abraham, Moses, David, Ruth, Esther, and Daniel, yet with the character judgment to be able to reject the enticing temptation of Lucifer "ye shall be as gods?"

How does God create a person like Paul, having the innate high intelligence and superb people-skills to fulfill the enormously difficult calling to evangelize the first-century Mediterranean world, yet possessing the humility to recognize, understand, and accept the loving intention of God wrapped up in the concept of "For I think that God hath set forth us, the apostles, last" (1 Corinthians 4:9).

The uniquely brilliant way that God has overcome this creative dilemma is to invent a vehicle called an *adventure of faith* involving the supernatural participation of God in the events and circumstances of our lives, centered around the timeless demonstration of perfect, unselfish love featured in the cross and resurrection of Jesus Christ. This is how God can supernaturally manufacture godly people who can make the character leap to becoming the father of faith, the governor of Egypt, a king of Israel, a missionary evangelist in the first century, or even the Son of God Himself flawlessly demonstrating these characteristics as the Lamb of God Savior for the entire world, without developing an inflated ego and a swelled head.

The people of faith in the Bible rise to the occasion of becoming capable of an intimate and fulfilling relationship with God amidst their God-composed life-scripts, without falling into the destructive self-worship of their own abilities and talents, because the adventure of faith invented by God

49

contains the element of seemingly insurmountable adversity which separates us from self-sovereignty. This accurately describes the life and ministry of Jesus Christ, and the essence of the cross.

The characters of faith in the Bible cannot reach their destinations through worldly conventional scenarios. It is the uniquely supernatural elements of the cross applied to the events in our lives that produces the God-desired outcome of gifted and talented people that God can have meaningful fellowship with, who also independently understand and appreciate the issues behind freely choosing righteousness and self-sacrificing love, instead of self-centered, self-worship.

This is the narrow-gate aspect of the cross of Jesus Christ that is inaccessible and incomprehensible to the world. Fulfilling our calling like Joseph, David, and Paul is not accomplished by going around God in a self-autonomous, worldly conventional effort. Nothing supernatural happens using this approach. Fulfilling our unique callings and actualizing God's intended character growth for each one of us, no matter what our particular gifts, talents, and circumstances, is accomplished by going directly through God. It is the supernatural participation of God in the circumstances and events of our lives, above and beyond conventional wisdom, that adds the purpose, meaning, and richness to a walk of faith with Jesus Christ.

A biblical quality journey of faith removes the element of pride because it is God's plan, not ours. There is no room for knee-jerk pushback, stubborn resistance to change, or the prideful protection of our established turf of doing things our way, when we surrender our leadership position to God as commander of the expedition. When our plans are entirely displaced by God-composed life-scripts, we follow God's leadership in faith and trust that leaves no room for pride-filled self-adulation.

As previewed in the God-composed life-scripts of the people of faith in the Bible, the end-times Christian church needs to become last, like Paul, within the seemingly impossible context of the tribulation events (Matthew 24:9-14; John 16:33) to be able to experience and exhibit the divine character traits of humility, love, forbearance, and forgiveness. At the beginning of the end-times tribulation, the Christian church does not need escape. At the beginning of the tribulation the church needs the supernatural infusion of God in our lives that will produce the biblical quality of faith that can say along with Job: "Though he slay me, yet will I trust him" (Job 13:15).

50

Paul's statement in this obscure and seldom taught 1 Corinthians 4:9 verse about his thinking that God has set forth himself and his colleagues the apostles as last, is actually one of the most powerful and instructive statements in all of the Bible. Paul is most effective in his outreach of the transforming power of the gospel message that can change a person from a life of sin and darkness into a new creature "in Christ" full of spiritual light and love, when Paul himself is least worldly-esteemed as an earthen clay pot emptied of the self-adoration of his own gifts and talents. Paul is operating at his highest and best use for service in the kingdom of God, filled with the power of the Holy Spirit, when God has set him forth in the eyes of the world as last. This is one of the keys to understanding our spiritual condition in the last-days when Christian will be hated of all nations (Matthew 24:9) and when the Spirit will be poured out upon all flesh (Joel 2:28-29).

Chapter Nine

The Two Advents of the Messiah

And Paul, as his manner was, went in unto them, and three sabbath days
reasoned with them out of the scriptures, Opening and alleging that Christ must
needs have suffered, and risen again from the dead; and that this Jesus, whom I
preach unto you, is Christ.   Acts 17:2-3

In Acts 13:14-41, Paul would have preferred to preach the outwardly
positive message of Jesus Christ the Messiah who rules and reigns from
Jerusalem as the political, spiritual, and military leader who would bring world
peace according to the prophecies we now understand in hindsight to relate to
the second advent of Christ. To begin his major evangelical missionary
outreach to the first-century Mediterranean world, Paul would have liked to
bring the welcome news to the Jews in the synagogue in Antioch Pisidia, of a
Messiah in Jerusalem who was in the beginning process of restoring their
homeland of Israel to political independence and spiritual predominance as in
centuries past. This is the message that all Jews living outside of Israel would
have been overjoyed to hear.

But Paul preached to them the cross (Mark 9:12). Paul (a Jew having a
first-rate rabbinical education, taught by Gamaliel in Jerusalem), preached that
Jesus the Messiah was crucified and rose from the dead (Acts 13:30) for the
remission of our sins (Acts 13:38-39), despite the temporary humiliation for our
sakes of becoming a curse hanged on a tree (Galatians 3:13). Paul preached the
message of the cross, which was an offense to many of the Jews of his day,
because they were looking in expectation for the other messiah, the "Son of
David" prophesied in the Old Testament who would redeem Israel from her
enemies and usher in an everlasting world reign of righteousness, justice, and
peace (1 Chronicles 17:11-13).

The Old Testament messianic prophecies that apply to the second
coming of Christ are in the Bible for a very good reason. They supply
indispensable information that forms the basis for hope for the future. But these
messianic prophecies also bring to the first century a razor-sharp sword for
dividing truth from error, and for exposing what is in the hearts of people, which
can be instructive for us today.

Paul wrote of the Jews of his day in Romans 10:3…"For they, being ignorant of God's righteousness, and going about to establish their own righteousness, have not submitted themselves unto the righteousness of God." Simeon in the temple in Jerusalem prophesied to Joseph and Mary: "Behold, this child is set for the fall and rising again of many in Israel; and for a sign which shall be spoken against (Yea, a sword shall pierce through thy own soul also), that the thoughts of many hearts may be revealed" (Luke 2:34-35). Jesus said of many of the Jews in Israel "And ye will not come to me, that ye might have life," and "How can ye believe, *who receive honor one of another*, and seek not the honor that cometh from God only?" (John 5:40; 5:44, italics mine).

Many of the Jews sitting in the audience in the synagogue in Antioch Pisidia, listening to Paul in Acts 13, thought of themselves, on balance, as good people. They did not think they needed additional spiritual improvement. They thought that they were righteous before God because they were Jews, faithfully practicing the Law and observing the rituals given to them by Moses. Their expectation was for a messiah who would fix the negative circumstances of their outside world, not reform their inner man through conviction of sin, repentance, and spiritual rebirth (John 3:3). This important distinction is the issue that Jesus emphasized in His famous night conversation with Nicodemus the Pharisee.

The new preaching of Paul and Barnabas in Antioch Pisidia exposed the fact that some practicing Jews, going through the mere outward motions of religious observances, were worshipping God for naught. Along these lines, Paul explains in Romans 9:6 "For they are not all Israel, who are of Israel." Paul goes on to say in Romans 11:2 that: "God hath not cast away his people whom he foreknew" and in the previous verse says that he himself is also a Jew, believing in Jesus Christ as the Messiah and Savior. Paul and Barnabas, both Jews, preached Jesus Christ crucified and risen from the grave for the remission of our sins into a new and living way.

This new gospel message exposed the large gulf between people performing religious practices in a purely mechanical exercise according to cultural expectations, without their heart and mind being truly committed and engaged, and a genuine journey of faith following Jesus Christ through unconventional life-scripts composed by God to reveal Himself individually to people. This was described by Jeremiah as the new covenant (Jeremiah 31:31-34). The *new covenant* preaching of Paul and Barnabas in Antioch Pisidia brought the journey-of-faith experience back full-circle to the promise of God to make Abraham, the father of faith, a blessing to all nations (Genesis 12:3; 22:18).

Jews and Gentiles alike, sitting together two thousand years later in the synagogue in Antioch Pisidia, fulfilled this ancient promise. The transition from the old covenant to the new covenant, inaugurating the new church age, exposed the emptiness of religious practices performed solely to enjoy the benefits of conforming to cultural expectations. The new covenant opened wide the already existing entrance into a life of faith in God first introduced through the life of faith of Abraham in Canaan years before, and perfected through the death and resurrection of Jesus Christ the Lamb of God sacrificed for our sins.

How a Partially Fulfilled Advent Becomes a Stumbling Stone

Some Jews in Antioch Pisidia did not accept Paul's gospel message of salvation through faith in Jesus Christ as Messiah, demonstrating what Simeon had accurately prophesied about the mixed reception a new covenant journey of faith, made accessible now through Christ to every new believer, would receive.

This is why Paul refers to the cross as an offense and a stumbling block unto the Jews (2 Corinthians 5:7; 1 Corinthians 1:23). Many Jews in the first century thought that all God had to do was repair their political/economic situation according to their understanding and expectations for the coming messiah, and then all would be well. They were already mistakenly self-righteous and saw no need for further spiritual reformation in their lives. They were spiritually blind to the coming of a more broadly accessible new covenant adventure of faith available to both Jews and Gentiles alike. Because their religious experience was limited to rituals and ceremonies only, and not a living and vibrant life of faith following God, they could not imagine a new covenant expanding to encompass the Gentile world, based upon the ancient prophecies surrounding Abraham the father of faith.

The direct and intimate participation of God in the events and circumstances of the lives of people of faith on a universal scale is made possible by the death and resurrection of Jesus of Nazareth during His first advent as Messiah. This is what Paul and Barnabas preached in Antioch Pisidia.

God wants to give us a tailor-made adventure of faith, because in doing so He gives us a revelation of Himself. Unless God shakes up our world, in the unconventionally biblical way of injecting Himself into the course of our lives to match on some level the experiences of the people of faith recorded in the Bible, we cannot experience the power of God's presence working through us. This salvation entrance through the cross of Christ leading into an unconventional adventure of faith, previewed long before in the life of Abraham, was just as desperately needed in an ongoing basis in the first century as it is still today in our own twenty-first century.

Paul was God's chosen mouthpiece based in large part upon the huge gulf between the true and the false in Paul's own past experience in mistakenly persecuting the early church. The outpouring of God's forgiving grace upon Paul at Damascus translated perfectly into the gospel outreach to the equally misguided polytheistic pagan culture of the Greco-Roman world. Paul's new covenant message contained a very large dose of giving up our old misguided way for God's correct new way. Back then as today, this was not clearly apparent, understood, or welcomed by everyone in Antioch Pisidia.

By contrast, the few Gentile "God-fearers" listening to Paul's opening message in the synagogue in Antioch Pisidia (recorded in Acts 13) about Jesus the crucified and risen Savior for the remission of sin, had no interest in the political and economic fortunes of the small and obscure Roman-occupied nation of Israel. To the Gentiles convicted of their sin nature through the Holy Spirit preaching of Paul, the immediate concern was not the restoration of Israel, but the restoration of their lost souls.

This same condition persists to our day. Many Jews today reject Jesus of Nazareth as a viable candidate for messiah, based solely upon a mistaken belief that He failed to fulfill the Old Testament messianic prophesies regarding the setting up of a glorious earthly rule and reign in Jerusalem, to end disease, evil, suffering, and sin in our present world. Many of the Jews in the first century were deeply disappointed in Jesus of Nazareth because they mistakenly combined all of the promises and expectations of the messianic prophesies into one single advent (Isaiah 9:6-7).

Many of the Jews of that day did not comprehend, accept, or practice personalized belief in God as patterned in the Old Testament examples of journeys-of-faith based upon God's intimate participation in our lives, in contrast to their more familiar experience of pursuing righteousness by the works of the law according to their own self-directed religious observances (John 5:42; Romans 10:3). Paul's message of deliverance from the bondage of self-sovereignty through the liberty of the cross of Jesus Christ was just as foreign sounding to some of the Jews in the first century as it is to worldly-minded people today.

As recorded in the Old Testament, God asked Noah, Abraham, Joseph, Moses, David, Samuel, Gideon, Esther and Mordecai, Elijah, and Daniel, to name a few, to do the difficult and hard thing, often at the risk of their lives. If Jesus had commenced His full reign in Jerusalem in the first century, without any personal sacrifice of His own, He would have assumed an elevated position of power on top of the backs of other people's self-sacrifices. With the benefit of clear hindsight today, the basic management principle of leading by example should have been obvious to the Jewish scholars, theologians, and rulers in first century Israel as they attempted to interpret messianic prophecy. But this true spiritual insight requires a personal experience following God equivalent to the positive journeys of faith recorded in the Bible, to be able to see and understand this fundamental leadership-based prerequisite.

The first advent of the messiah had to conform to the Psalms 22 and Isaiah 53 picture of a suffering servant, according to the universally recognized virtue of a leader never asking people to do something they themselves would not do. Jesus setting up His earthly reign in Jerusalem in the first century would have been disappointingly inconsistent with what God had been doing in Israel through the lives of people of faith, during the previous two thousand years. Jesus beginning His reign prior to experiencing the cross would have been below the high standards God sets for Himself, and below the high standards God had asked of people up to that point in time.

Jesus was about to ask his disciples over the next two thousand years to also do the hard and difficult thing, often again at the risk of their lives. Perfect divine virtue required Jesus Christ to go before us in this aspect of choosing the hard and difficult way for the advancement of truth. Most of the people in Israel missed this logical separation of the two advents of the messiah, because they themselves were not personally engaged in a biblical journey of faith following God's lead that might have illuminated this basic leadership principle.

What is it that we want in our Relationship with God?

Christian philosophy and apologetics has rightly clarified a key distinction about faith in the existence of God. Real faith in God does not exist

56

in a world in which the existence of God is an absolute observable fact like the existence of the noonday sun, or an undisputable truth like two plus two equals four. Over the previous six thousand or more years of human redemptive history, God has skillfully maintained a delicate balance between the evidence for His existence and the ability of humans to exercise unbelief. This keeps in play the critical element of free-will choice, which adds value and meaning to our choice to trust and follow God in faith, in this broken world.

The key point that many Jews in the first century blindly missed in evaluating Jesus of Nazareth as a candidate for messiah, is that Jesus ruling and reigning on earth in the fullest sense, starting sometime around 30 to 33 A.D., brings to an abrupt end the exercise of free-will choice and the experience of a journey of faith. They missed this key point because they themselves had not experienced a personal journey of faith with God in their own lives (John 7:17). God's ability to compose and orchestrate brilliantly original life-scripts to reveal Himself to people who choose to follow Him through the medium of an adventure of faith, ends abruptly in this current broken world environment when Jesus permanently assumes His place on the throne as King and Savior according to the second advent half of the messianic prophecies.

Gideon's experience of an Old Testament challenge of faith, recorded in the book of Judges, would have had no further context to play itself out in Christ's glorious reign…there will be no Midianites or anyone else attacking the New Jerusalem then or forever after. The type of brilliantly creative journey of faith of Joseph's rise in Egypt, recorded in the Old Testament book of Genesis, would have no further context to actualize in Christ's glorious rule and reign upon earth…there will be no more famines in Egypt or anywhere else from that time onward. If the messianic prophecies of the first and second advent of Jesus Christ are fully combined in the first century, the powerful conversion and subsequent ministry of Paul has no continuing context…no one, including Paul, would mistakenly be persecuting the early church during Christ's rule and reign in the first century.

The fulfillment of the second-advent portions of the messianic prophecies regarding Jesus Christ, and all that they entail, would have been totally premature in the first century. The human race was not ready for the fulfillment of these final messianic prophecies. Many of the chosen people of God…the Jews in the first century…did not at that time understand the concepts of grace, a journey of faith, or the Old Testament verse that "the just shall live by faith" (Habakkuk 2:4) that Paul clarified in his New Testament writings and that Martin Luther rediscovered at the beginning of the Protestant Reformation. Even to this day, contemporary Christianity has still not fully recovered an understanding and worldly-free application of the second half of the cross in the lives of individual born-again Christians, which was partially lost during the dark and middle ages of history.

Jesus said that He had more lost sheep, not of this first century fold, to seek and to save (John 10:16). This meant that God had many more individualized, unconventional life-scripts to compose and orchestrate as only God can do, to personally reveal Himself to the people of faith to come into existence during the centuries of the church age. Christianity moves out from the purity of doctrine and practice in Judea into the paganism and classical philosophy of the Greco-Roman world, especially after the destruction of Jerusalem in 70 A.D., so that mankind can work through the eternally important issues of truth for the next 1900 years or more. This all-important task is still ongoing.

There were tens of thousands of first century Jews in Jerusalem, in Israel, and in the Mediterranean world who did accept Jesus as Messiah and believed in Him as Savior (Acts 2:41; Acts 4:4; Acts 21:20). But there obviously was a large difference in the first century between the backgrounds, cultures, and expectations of the Jews and the Gentiles. The Gentiles had no expectations about any messiah whatsoever...world ruler or suffering servant...because a gospel message regarding the fulfillment of age-old biblical messianic prophecies was entirely unknown to them.

The Gentile Christians of the New Testament era therefore had no reason to be offended by a crucified and risen Jesus Christ as Messiah. The Gentiles in the first century Greco-Roman world, who were moved by the Holy Spirit preaching of Paul, gladly received the gospel message by faith because they recognized their personal sin and their need for a Savior. The Gentiles in Antioch Pisidia believed the message of Paul, wanted to become new creatures in Christ, and recognized their need to discard their past lives of sin through the cross.

The Gentiles who believed the preaching of Paul were open to the idea of a new adventure of faith following Jesus Christ according to the new covenant model of a personal relationship with God. In this sense they were no different from the Jews in Antioch Pisidia who also believed and accepted this message of salvation through the preaching of Christ crucified and risen,

58

introduced by Paul and Barnabas. *From this moment forward, both Jews and Gentiles entered into the new covenant adventures of faith that God would compose and orchestrate for each one of them.* This fulfilled the prophetic promise of God to Abraham, and is described by Paul in Romans 10:12.

The preaching of the cross by Paul in Antioch Pisidia in Acts thirteen, to begin his lifelong ministry of evangelism to the first century Mediterranean world, divides and separates forever the difference between the unconventional nature of a God-composed life-script entered through faith in Christ, and the empty and lifeless performance of perfunctory religious practices not having the intimate participation of the living God in the events and circumstances of our lives. If people are indeed made complete in our new covenant relationship with God, if being "in Christ" is the truest form of rational existence, then the preaching of Paul in Antioch Pisidia is a demonstration of the component of pure, divinely unselfish love intended to seek and to save that which is lost (Matthew 18:11). This extends down through the centuries as the love-filled component of the high standards of God for the soon coming end-times.

Christians living today in the developed nations of the world are in danger of falling into a subtle variation of the same mistake the Jews made in the first century in rejecting Jesus of Nazareth as their Messiah. If our vision is worldly horizontal only, if we are looking for a Jesus who will fix our outward world by providing a better job, a bigger house, a nicer car, better vacations, and more economic wealth and prosperity, based solely on performing religious observances and church attendance, then we are once again repeating history and looking for the wrong messiah. If we are going through the motions of attending church solely for the benefits of fitting-in and conforming to the social and cultural expectations of our immediate family and/or our local community, then we are in jeopardy of being left behind as were the Jews in Antioch Pisidia, who were exposed by Paul's message of a new covenant adventure of faith through Christ (Acts 13:39). We are in jeopardy of likewise being identified as merely a lukewarm religious person participating in the synagogue for all of the wrong reasons.

If we are looking for a soft and malleable God who will stay safely within the boundary limits of conventional religious normalcy in His participation and impact upon our lives, then we are looking for a God who is not the God of the Bible.

59

Modern Christians must choose Jesus Christ for the same correct reason the Jews and Gentiles received Paul's message in Antioch Pisidia in the first century. Paul preached the cross and the resurrection because it is the *power of God* to change a person from a life of sin to a life of righteousness, faith, and holiness. Paul could preach with bold conviction the transforming power of the cross and the resurrection of Christ, because Paul stood before the crowd of people in the synagogue in Antioch Pisidia as a living example of this transformation.

The message of the cross leads directly to an unconventional, individually scripted adventure of faith following Jesus Christ, to match the journey of faith that Paul was personally experiencing and preaching about in Antioch Pisidia. The same separation from the worldly conventional in the first century exists today, with the precise details of our new-covenant Christian lives varying to match our own individual God-given talents and modern-day callings.

People who are justified in their own self-estimation, who think they are just fine the way they are, who have no interest in pursuing an adventure of faith in fellowship with the living God, will look for a God who will fix their outer worldly circumstances only.

Adam and Eve had everything in the Garden of Eden. They were in idyllic surroundings of incomparable beauty, and they enjoyed daily fellowship with God Himself. But when they were tempted with *having more*…to become "as gods, knowing good and evil," they disobeyed God and fell into sin. They succumbed to the enticement of *having more*.

In Mark 14:53-65 and Matthew 26:57-66, during His night trial before Caiaphas the high priest and some of the scribes and Jewish elders, Jesus is asked "are you the messiah, tell us plainly?" Jesus is the personification of Isaiah 9:6-7, the Son of God in a human body, as He humbly stands on trial before this group of religious leaders in Jerusalem. Yet clearly He is not up to their expectations. They *wanted more*. Jesus was not out in battle with an Israeli army defeating the Romans. Jesus was not rallying the populace toward the political and economic reforms that would beneficially change the entire world. Jesus was not in the process of restoring the old glory and splendor of the reigns of David and Solomon, which would beneficially spill over into the power base of these religious rulers. Jesus was not even verbally defending Himself, in fulfillment of the prophecy in Isaiah 53:7.

Jesus instead had been out in the countryside of Israel amongst the common people, healing the sick, casting out demons, teaching eternal truths, and raising the dead. He was eternally impacting people's lives. Jesus was doing in the first century what He is still doing today…beneficially transforming people through deliverance from sin, creating spiritual rebirth, and building growth in character that comes through a journey of faith actively following God.

As Jesus stands before these religious leaders of Israel, Jesus models this unconventional life-script of God perfectly (Isaiah 55:8-9). The life-script of God for Jesus of Nazareth, the Lamb of God Savior slain from the foundation of time for the sins of mankind (Revelation 13:8), is composed and orchestrated by God the Father to perfectly match the uniquely divine capacity of the Son of God. In rejecting Jesus, these men are not only rejecting the physical manifestation of God Himself standing before them, but they are also emphatically rejecting the God-composed, supernaturally unconventional journey-of-faith exemplified in Jesus that makes Him uniquely the way, the truth, and the life.

These religious leaders did not want the way, the truth, and the life through a God-composed, unconventional adventure of faith that would separate them from the pride of their own self-sovereignty. These religious leaders wanted a God who would only intervene in the external world according to their partially incomplete interpretation of the messianic prophecies, while leaving in place their ability to operate as the autonomous gods of their lives.

This is one of the powerful motivating forces explaining the reason why these religious leaders went to such extreme lengths to unwittingly, unknowingly, and personally fulfill the messianic prophecies by having Jesus the Messiah crucified. It is ironically fitting that through their dual rejection of Jesus and a God-composed journey-of-faith, they themselves directly provided the very means by which God opened up the way of salvation through Christ's atoning sacrifice on the cross. This is why the cross is such a deadly serious issue, surgically dividing truth from error, and demonstrates why God our Father cannot successfully be fooled with, outwitted, or outmaneuvered.

Jesus was indeed offering more, but it was on a higher level incomprehensible to these religious leaders. Jesus was offering to them, to the nation of Israel, and to us today, a life-experience comparable to that of

Abraham, Joseph, Moses, David, and what was to be experienced in the very near future in the lives of Peter, Paul, and the early church.

The "more" that Jesus was offering rises above the unsatisfying possession of an abundance of material objects, that will rust and decay here on earth. The "more" that Jesus was offering surpasses the fickleness of worldly applause and acclaim, which can quickly fade from memory and turn overnight into jeers and rejection. Jesus was offering no less than the personal working and moving of the Almighty Creator of the universe in our lives to craft us into people who can exhibit and enjoy the benefits of unselfish love, forgiveness of others, the satisfaction of commendable industry and excellence in our work, and the rock-solid confidence of elevated character that nothing and no one on this earth can overturn.

Jesus was offering to these religious leaders and to us, a transformed new life that can be elevated up into the unconventional, supernatural workings of God that can craft Joseph into the governor of Egypt, David into the king of Israel, and can completely change a person like Saul of Tarsus into the Apostle Paul of the book of Acts and Romans chapter sixteen.

A Perfect Balance of the Cross and the Resurrection

The gospel message has a powerful positive appeal to it, of the real hope of a life-transforming change for people, whether it is spoken by John the Baptist at the Jordan river, by Jesus to the woman at the well (John 4:5-45), by Peter to the multitudes at Pentecost, or by Paul to the Jews and Gentiles in Antioch Pisidia. This preaching of the gospel message comes within a confident, bold, selfless, truth-piercing delivery of genuine conviction out of Holy Spirit inspired purity of heart. This is one of the invaluable pay-offs for the Christian disciple picking up their cross and patiently following Jesus through an adventure of faith. The ability to someday share our testimony with natural simplicity, with the power of honest conviction, with the freedom of complete unawareness of self in fearless love, and with complete mastery over the opposing spirit of unbelief, to family, friends, neighbors, and co-workers, is an outcome of the cross and the resurrection in our lives that is of incalculable worth.

Paul preached the cross in Antioch Pisidia. This is still the central, key issue of our present-day Christian experience. How do we define the person of Jesus Christ, and what do we expect in our relationship with Him? Are we

62

looking for a similarly unconventional, God-composed experience like that of Abraham? Are we willing to risk everything like Joseph to discover for ourselves that God is trustworthy and true, and to be used mightily for others? Can God call us like Moses to go to Egypt, so to speak, in our modern world context to share our Christian testimony to deliver the captives from the bondage of sin?

Can we follow God to the banks of the Red Sea, patiently looking to God in faith and trust to manufacture a miraculous deliverance in the face of seemingly insurmountable challenge? Can we relate to Paul, who said that the world was crucified unto him, and he unto the world (Galatians 6:14)? Is our personal relationship with Jesus Christ the most important thing in our lives? Or are we looking merely for a messiah who will temporarily repair our outward world only, while at the same time allowing us to remain as sovereign kings atop the thrones of our lives?

The totally unexpected separation in the first century of the coming of the messiah as prophesied in Isaiah 9:6-7, Genesis 3:15, and Jeremiah 33:15-16, for example, into two distinct advents accomplishing two entirely different tasks, was and is one of the great issues of the first-century ministry of Jesus Christ. This separation exposed and divided out of the body of believers those Jews who were merely going through the mechanical, perfunctory motions of synagogue worship. It inaugurated the living new covenant relationship with God that made the journey-of-faith experiences of Abraham, Joseph, Moses, David, Daniel, and Elijah available and commonplace for every new covenant Christian, Jew and Gentile alike. And it created the church age that has continued down twenty centuries to our present time.

This unexpected and unanticipated split into two messianic advents had enormous ramifications for the human race. It perpetuated the intense hatred of the Jews toward the occupying Romans, eventually resulting in the destruction of Jerusalem in A.D. 70 and the scattering of the Jews around the world for 1,900 years. The first advent of Jesus Christ as Savior kept in play the adventure of faith for countless people for another 2,000 years, and produced the colorful history of the church age through the dark and middle ages, through the Reformation, and through the incredible and remarkable past four centuries of recent history.

The gospel message of the cross preached by Paul in Antioch Pisidia, leading to a biblical-quality adventure of faith, is staring us in the face today as much as ever. This timely truth is right there in front of us…so close we can reach out and grab it for ourselves. The best and finest life is the uniquely unconventional life of faith that God has composed and would orchestrate for us, to match the pattern and template recorded in the Bible, however and wherever that takes us. We have all the evidence we need to step out in faith, place our trust in Jesus Christ, and begin our journey toward whatever lies ahead in the upcoming last-days.

Chapter Ten

Spiritual Opposition

And the rain descended, and the floods came, and the winds blew and beat upon that house, and it fell not; for it was founded upon a rock.   Matthew 7:25

Spiritual opposition to people living and walking in the Spirit is a reality previewed for us in the Bible (Ephesians 6:12). Opposition in the form of negative situations and circumstances in the natural realm is one way that spiritual darkness sows doubts, creates fears, undermines resolve, attacks faith, and weakens trust within the active servants of God. Spiritual darkness can even use negative situations and circumstances to retaliate against the servants of God, after the fact when God has wrought some positive spiritual work through them, large or small.

God allows spiritual darkness to operate within the natural realm of events and circumstances. God is so intelligent He can reshape the efforts of spiritual opposition into re-directed positive outcomes for believers who are in the midst of God-composed and orchestrated walks of faith. The reason that "all things work together for good to them that love God, to them who are the called according to his purpose" (Romans 8:28) is that God is smarter than the agents of evil. In the Bible, God always takes spiritual opposition that presents itself in the form of negative appearing events and circumstances, and turns this spiritual opposition around for good outcomes when faith and trust in Him are in operation.

Lucifer introduced evil into the world in the Garden of Eden. God is not the author of this evil. God has been demonstrating His divine quality ever since that time, through His ability to take evil and reshape it for His good purposes. This is one of the most powerful lessons in the Bible. Throughout the biblical record of God's interaction with man, God refocuses evil in the direction He wants it to go, defeats it, creates an object lesson out of the encounter, and generates beneficial spiritual growth for His followers all in one brilliant stroke. We see this repeated many times in the Old and New Testaments of the Bible.

The example of Joseph being sold into slavery to a caravan heading for Egypt, by his brothers, was meant for evil. God took this evil action and turned it around for good on a massive scale. Who other than God could compose such a story as Joseph's, in which everyone, including Joseph, required hindsight in looking back at events to be able to understand and appreciate what God had done?

The cross of Jesus Christ is the ultimate example of this divine ability to shape and remold spiritual opposition into a beneficial outcome, in this case the sacrificial redemption of mankind from the curse of sin through the exercise of faith in Christ. The cross and the resurrection tell us that God can take evil in its deadliest form, and turn it upside down on its head to perform a great work of God in complete frustration of evil's original intent.

When God is in charge of the program, spiritual opposition loses every time. God is so intelligent He uses the very deception that Lucifer originally devised in the Garden of Eden to attempt to undermine God's authority, to instead illuminate the spiritually bankrupt nature of sin and thereby our deep need for God. God is so intelligent He uses the spiritual opposition intended to trip up the Christian, instead as actual lesson-plans to divide for us the difference between right and wrong. These lesson-plans help us to discover genuine repentance in the character areas we are deficient…short temper, impatience, pride. God is so intelligent He can take the evil opposition that is intended to destroy us and creatively use it to help us to grow spiritually strong into Christ-like character and conduct. God set up this physical environment called earth, knowing that this was the best possible environment for exercising faith and trust in Him through situations and circumstances that both spiritual darkness and spiritual light had an opportunity to utilize. The God of the Bible is never intimidated, deterred, or outsmarted by spiritual darkness, no matter how deceptive or terrifying it seems in the natural realm of events and circumstances.

Isaiah 9:6 gives many names for Jesus Christ…Wonderful, Counselor, The Mighty God, The Everlasting Father, and The Prince of Peace. Jesus, the Prince of Peace, cannot remove the offenses of this world until all of the purposes of God are completed. But Jesus can change evil into outcomes of eternal peace because He is both God and the Prince of Peace. Jesus Christ can superimpose peace in and through any set of circumstances concocted by spiritual darkness when people place their faith and trust in Him. Five of the most important words ever written are found in Psalm 23:4…"for thou art with me." God's promise to keep safe His faithful followers is based upon His love *and* His mastery over spiritual opposition.

Paul is nearly stoned to death by the Jews in Lystra (Acts 14:19) because Paul and Barnabas are being used of God mightily to convert the Gentiles to the new Christian faith. Yet Paul is not defeated by this extreme opposition to his ministry. On the contrary, as a result of this stoning, Paul is probably freer of any remaining inhibitions about preaching the gospel, is more determined than ever not to be defeated, and is further stripped of his self-in-control nature. Paul could add this new experience of a near-death stoning to his resume as an apostle, suffering in conformity to the cross of Christ as a definite sign that his ministry was having an impact (Ephesians 5:20).

Stephen is martyred by the Jews of Jerusalem because He is defending the new way of Jesus Christ as the risen Messiah with such power and persuasiveness (Acts 6:10) that the Sanhedrin cannot tolerate Stephen's message in their city. But spiritual opposition does not win in this confrontation with Stephen. Stephen does give his life as a faithful witness to Jesus Christ. But as Stephen was about to be stoned to death, Acts 7:55 says that he looked up into heaven and saw "the glory of God, and Jesus standing on the right hand of God."

Acts 8:1-4 then goes on to describe how an intensified persecution of the Christian church after this stoning of Stephen, resulted in the church being scattered to outlying regions around Jerusalem and as far away as Phoenicia, Cyprus, and Antioch (Acts 11:19), creating the first Christian missionaries. Spiritual opposition silenced Stephen, but in doing so it set in motion the persecution spearheaded by the young Saul soon-to-become Paul, and thereby created the opposite unintended consequence of hundreds of Christian missionaries who "went everywhere preaching the word" (Acts 8:4). God took Stephen's sacrifice at the hands of spiritual opposition, and turned it into the beneficial pattern of missionary evangelism that would continue down to our present day.

Peter is arrested by Herod the king, and scheduled for martyrdom to politically appease the Jewish rulers (Acts 12:3-4) This was in opposition to the great work that the Holy Spirit was doing through Peter and the other apostles in the growing Christian church in Jerusalem. This spiritual opposition that manifested itself in the outer natural realm, first in the execution by Herod of the Apostle James (Acts 12:2), then in the seemingly hopeless outward appearance of doom for Peter, did not deter God in the slightest. God simply reached deeper into His assortment of options and sent one of His angels to release Peter and guide him safely out of the prison. Scripture does not tell us why God allowed James to be killed at this time. But we can be sure that after Peter's rescue, the second rescue from prison in his Christian career (Acts 5:19), that even the heretofore highly experienced Apostle Peter gained a greater confidence in yielding and surrendering himself into the care of the Almighty God.

The Old and New Testaments of the Bible are filled with similar stories of situations and circumstances meant to destroy God's people or individual servants of God, which God then channels and re-directs towards a good outcome containing positive spiritual lessons and character-building. Equally important, the Old Testament tells us that God is capable of using spiritual opposition on a macro scale, in the form of the threat of invading foreign armies, periods of exile, captivities, and dispersions, to redirect the entire nation of Israel back into the sphere of His ways.

This is one of the upcoming great issues of our time…that God is so in control of events and circumstances that He can beneficially use evil and spiritual opposition as tools to reveal His divine capacity to resolve a crisis and work His purposes at the same time. The Christian, who has learned through a walk of faith, that in a God-led life all things work together for good, will not be deterred, offended, or discouraged by the spiritual opposition that will manifest itself in the natural realm of events in the upcoming last days (Matthew 24:6).

Whether it is Daniel in the lion's den, or Shadrach, Meshach, and Abednego in the fiery furnace, or Queen Esther trusting in God's protective care in approaching the king in opposition to Haman the powerful enemy of her people, God is able to combine overcoming victory, the dividing of truth from error, and beneficial spiritual growth within each of His masterfully creative solutions. The character traits of unconditional forgiveness and unselfish love exhibited in the believer through the heart and mind of Christ, *cannot be defeated* under any set of dire circumstances (Luke 23:34).

Like the fruits of the Spirit, against such there is no law (Galatians 5:22), the traits of perfect love and Christ-like character are not subject to defeat (1 John 5:4). In a world where Spirit-born Christians already possess eternal life, the character traits of faithfulness, fidelity, trust, and loving commitment to Christ eventually win-out, even in martyrdom. In a world where Jesus is risen from the death of the cross, Christians do not have to be afraid of anyone or anything (2 Timothy 1:7). The willingness to become as last (1 Corinthians 4:9), and to be fashioned as empty vessels able to contain the outpouring of the

68

Spirit for ministry in the last days (Joel 2:28-29), will set apart the end-times Christian in glorious revelation of the character of Jesus Christ at the end of human redemptive history.

The Bible teaches us that the condition of mankind, while lost in sin, is out of balance (Ephesians 2:1). God created mankind with the capacity to live as human beings, not as gods unto themselves. When a person repents and accepts Christ into their lives, they step down off the throne of their hearts to give place for God to assume His correct position in the relationship. This is one of the explanations for why people, who become born-again in the Spirit, experience a deep inner sense of joy, peace, and relief. They no longer have to assume the unnatural role of being the god that they were not created to be. The blood that Jesus shed on the cross not only washes the repentant believer clean of sin, but also sets in proper order and balance Jesus Christ on the throne of a person's life. The born-again Christian, who has vacated the throne of their heart to make room at the top for God, can venture out into a genuine walk of faith *following* Jesus Christ, *precisely because they are now operating as a human being and not as a god.*

Following Jesus is the Pinnacle of Human Experience

Lucifer takes the Christian born-again salvation experience and slanders it with one of his most deceptive lies. The world accuses the new Christian of having a weak character, of copping-out, of using God as a crutch, by relinquishing their throne and giving it over to Jesus Christ as Lord and Master. This is the crux, the heart of the issue over sin. Lucifer tells man to remain in his fallen nature as a god on the throne of his life. But man was not created with the capacity to be a god. God is the only person qualified to sit on a spiritual throne. When we push God away and continue to assume the unnatural position of being our own gods, we are spiritual rebels. Lucifer has led mankind to join his rebellion by getting us to think we are something we are not. Lucifer has deceptively gotten mankind to accept a job promotion at a divine management level that we are not qualified nor trained for.

What is incredibly remarkable about this whole affair is that God's solution to the spiritual opposition of Lucifer fomenting rebellion within the ranks of mankind, once again is to brilliantly take spiritual darkness and turn it around upon itself. By enlisting mankind in his rebellion against God, Lucifer has unintentionally and unwittingly given God a wide-open door to expose for us the eternal key to peace and happiness. The way to eternal joy and peace is found in knowing who and what we were created to be within a relationship with the Almighty God, and not in attempting to be gods in autonomous rebellion outside of fellowship with God. We are in our most blessed condition when we are living securely within our capacity as human beings, allowing God to walk in the very large-sized shoes that only He is capable of filling. This is a formula that will happily work for us for all of eternity.

Lucifer introducing sin into the world, and God's illuminating answer to it, forever solidifies for us the eternal truth of being graciously, lovingly, unselfishly, and contentedly satisfied with being who and what we are within the context of our creation by God (1 Timothy 6:6). We can exercise the most brilliant and creative God-given attributes, safe from destructive pride for all eternity, as long as we stay within the parameters of loving thoughtfulness and beneficial service to others, thanks to this all-important spiritual lesson we learn here on earth. The divine character of the Holy Spirit living within the Christian makes this invaluable lesson...of death to our self-in-control natures through the cross, of the benefit of stepping down from the thrones of our hearts...accessible and comprehensible to us. The fact that God can craft this priceless lesson for us out of the challenging environment of spiritual darkness and rebellion validates forever God's claim to be a loving and all-wise God.

The power of Lucifer's deceptive lie about Christians being weak because we rely upon God instead of exclusively on ourselves, when turned on its head, supplies an opposite but equal force in God's rebuttal response. Stepping down off the throne of our lives opens up the opportunity for an adventurous, unconventional, supernatural walk of faith following Jesus Christ, which by God's intentional design contains genuine risk. Accepting the risk of failure following Jesus Christ through a walk of faith, having no advance guarantee of success other than the Word of God, our current relationship with God, and our previous positive Christian experiences, is the opposite of being weak. The step out of the familiarity of self-reliance into a new adventure of faith following God requires courage, not weakness.

The real truth is that there cannot be a risk/reward, courage filled walk-of-faith while we remain in the state of being our own god. Two kings cannot occupy the same throne. That is why repentance is not weakness but enlightened good sense. How can anyone trust Jesus Christ about things over which we still maintain complete control? Until we surrender as rebels and throw down our arms in this issue as to who should be God, eternal life in the Spirit in a proper relationship with God cannot begin.

Surrendering all to Jesus is the epitome of *stepping out* into an adventure of faith, in the one area that really counts for something…the course of our lives. The Christian walk of faith is the exact opposite of the lie that Lucifer spins about the weakness of the life following Jesus Christ, when Jesus is atop the throne of our heart. Stepping down off the throne of our heart, turning away from being our own god, and inviting Jesus Christ to assume His rightful place as God, is the foundational cornerstone truth that will set people free to enjoy a life of peace and fulfillment for all eternity.

In a nutshell, this is the *great end-times closing message.* People are not gods. We were never meant to be gods. We have no business being a part of Lucifer's rebellion. Lucifer is still trying to make his point in his rebellion, and he is using mankind as his foil, using people as his dupes. That is why it will be sheer lunacy to accept the end-times mark of the beast in allegiance to the Antichrist.

Jesus Christ selflessly died on the cross to set us free from ourselves in this deceptively miscast role of being our own gods. The Bible tells us we were created in the image of God, not actual gods ourselves. Jesus Christ really is the Way, the Truth, and the Life, because the walk of faith orchestrated by God for us through this current broken world begins by correctly enthroning Christ atop our lives. Jesus Christ is our Savior and King for a very simple and practical reason…He actually is God…we are not.

Chapter Eleven

The High Standards of God for End-Times Christians

Multitudes, multitudes in the valley of decision; for the day of the Lord is near
in the valley of decision.   Joel 3:14

What is at stake in these three key words that apply to Jesus being the
way, the *truth*, and the *life* (John 14:6)? Why write a book about the high
standards of God as we approach the beginning stages of the end-times?
Staying with the motion picture theme started in the first chapter, I will try to
briefly sum-up an answer to close out the book.

The part of the make-believe world of movie acting that is not make-
believe is the bond of friendship and camaraderie that is often formed within the
acting troop. The relationships between the fictional characters within the story
and the fictional world the actors are playing-out in the movie are oftentimes
better than the actor's real lives.

The invention of DVD movies that can be replayed in our television
sets has allowed for something called Special Features to be included that
contain interviews with the actors and the movie directors. Toward the end of
shooting on set, actors in recent movies like Pride and Prejudice (2005), or the
movie trilogy The Lord of the Rings (2003), for example, often say that they
enjoyed the friendships they formed while playing their fictional roles so much
that they wish their movie make-believe world would continue indefinitely.

This secular window into our human nature provides a glimpse into
something important about us. Well-written fictional characters, acted out
within movie-scripts having high ideals, with capable, talented, and caring
movie-directors, and supportive fellow actors, creates a short-lived, idyllic yet
challenging and fulfilling environment that we would popularly call "a small
slice of heaven on earth."

But this idea runs much deeper. Throughout the filming of a great
movie, in memorizing their lines, studying their characters, and acting their
parts, the actors must think about and internalize the issues of the story
composed within the artistic inspiration of the storywriter. This is also what
occurs in a journey of faith following Jesus Christ...we learn the deep and

fundamental issues of truth while living a walk of faith. Paul can write his New Testament letters by living the life Jesus composed for him as the missionary evangelist to the first-century Greco-Roman world.

What is different in our subordination of self in following the lead of Jesus the Great Director in our personal journeys of faith, and in the larger grand story of human redemptive history, is that it does not all come to an end with a "wrap" of the filming production and the actors finally going their separate ways. The bonds of friendship we form with God, and with other believers, last for eternity in a new heavenly world without time.

The improved character traits we purchase through a journey of faith actually take shape and become part of ourselves, not just in the form of the wisdom and knowledge that actors take with them after studying a particular character and learning their lines in order to act out that character in a fictional movie. The journey of faith, being led into all truth by the Holy Spirit according to Ephesians 2:10, results in us *becoming* the enhanced character of the story, rather than abandoning our movie-acting roles at the end of film shooting to return to our otherwise normal lives. Peter speaking to the Sanhedrin, or Paul addressing Festus, are not fictional roles...they are real, eternally beneficial character building performances.

An accomplished actor performs "in-the-moment" using their natural personalities and emotions, but empty of their true selves in favor of inhabiting and possessing the fictional character portion of the stage play or movie they are in. Great actors lose themselves in their character portrayal to the point that they temporarily suspend all sense of nervousness, stage-fright, and self-awareness. It is being empty of self, yet utilizing our own personality traits and emotions that create a memorable performance in terms of facial expressions, voice modulation, body motions, and interactions with the other actors. But at the close of each day of shooting on the set, actors revert back to their normal selves. Not so with Spirit-led Christians engaged in a God-composed walk of faith.

Partnership with the Holy Spirit producing beneficial character growth becomes permanently ours...becomes part of us. This is what God hopes and longs for...that we will become who and what He created us to be, living and acting voluntarily at a high moral level that He can relate to, enjoy, and be comfortable with forever, time without end. Isn't this a similar pattern to what we long for in our relationships with our own children and grandchildren?

73

The biblical journey of faith is the real performance that has lasting benefits and consequences beyond our current imaginations. Passing from death into eternal life is the raising of the curtain for the beginning of the actual stage-performance. This current rehearsal preparation to enter into a new world where time does not exist, fully trained and familiar with our true intended character roles "in-Christ" according to the script composed by the great Playwright God, elevates the process of *becoming* sons and daughters of God to the level of the High Standards of God for End-Times Christians.

The Bible does not tell us what heaven will be like. Words written in black letters on the white pages of a book could not adequately describe the marvels of heaven. But judging by the preview of this current physical earth that God created, and our own incredible motor skills, five senses, and intellectual curiosity, it is a safe, educated guess that heaven is likewise filled with a myriad of natural wonders, interesting and challenging activities, breath-taking places to visit, and fascinating people and heavenly creatures to meet.

God created us in His image. God created us with the capacity to be able to appreciate and enjoy an environment where friendship and love can exist for an eternity. Jesus Christ is the great Screenwriter of Life for all time and the Master Director of the ultimate movie-set. We would all like to spend each and every day of eternity being an integral, contributing, and valued member of His cast.

Lucifer isolated himself from God through his rebellion. Lucifer's malicious and wicked intent is to draw man away from God into isolation as well. Sin tragically separates us from God and from each other. What is at stake in this contest as to who controls the thrones of our hearts, is the fundamental meaning and purpose behind the existence of life.

The bond of friendship and love is one of the most satisfying things in existence. When the angels in heaven announced the birth of Christ in Bethlehem, they said "Glory to God in the highest, and on earth peace, good will toward men" (Luke 2:14). Jesus said: "I am come that they might have life and that they might have it more abundantly" (John 10:10). As Spirit-born Christians, we must enter into this living journey of faith that promotes a friendship with God and selfless camaraderie with other believers, that will surpass anything we might ask or think (Ephesians 3:20) in this life. And we must try, through the Holy Spirit inspired means of loving persuasion and the evidence of our own transformed lives, to bring in as many other people into this eternal joy and happiness as possible. This is a part of the divine motivation behind the high standards of God for end-times Christians.

There is an old saying: "If you aim for nothing, you are sure to hit it." The contemporary Christian church in the developed countries needs to refocus on the simplicity and purity of Christ, the cross, and the power of the resurrected life. We need leaders who will point people toward Christ, and a genuine, biblical walk of faith, so that the church can achieve the high standards that God intends for individuals and the body of Christ as a whole. If as Christians we lower our spiritual vision to the horizontal level of worldly acceptance and expectations instead of the cross and the narrow gate (Matthew 7:13-14), we aim at nothing and are guaranteed to hit it.

With God's leading, when we do finally discover the individual narrow way for us, establish our spiritual footing, and find our place of service in God's grand plan, God will say to us: "I always loved you and meant the very best for you. Thank you for trusting me enough to help you. I enjoyed the time I spent with you and am looking forward to knowing you throughout eternity."

We were created with the potential for a walk of faith with God. These are The High Standards of God in the End-Times for individual Christians and for His church as a whole. God is the only capable author and director of this process.

I hope this book was a blessing, an encouragement, and an inspiration to you.

Sinner's Prayer

If you would like to become a Christian, you can do so by asking Jesus Christ to come into your life by praying the following words:

Lord Jesus, I confess that I am a sinner. I ask that you forgive my sin. I believe you died on the cross and that you rose three days later from the grave. I surrender my life to you as my Lord and Savior. I invite you into my heart and life. Thank you for giving me eternal life. Thank you for the Holy Spirit who now lives inside me to help me become a new person in Christ. Be with me forever. Amen.

If you sincerely prayed these words in faith, then you are now a born-again Christian and a son or daughter of God (John 1:12). If you own a Bible, begin reading the New Testament gospels, beginning with Matthew, then Luke, and then the book of Acts. Begin to pray (speak with God) every day. Ask God to lead and guide you from this day forward. Seek fellowship with Bible-believing Christians. God bless you.

Printed in Great Britain
by Amazon